Reiki Healing Meditation for Beginners

Learn Reiki symbols, tips and Reduce Stress for one good meditation

By Robert Khatri

of inattention or otherwise, by any usage or abuse of any policies, processes, or directions contained within is the solitary and utter responsibility of the recipient reader. Under no circumstances will any legal responsibility or blame be held against the publisher for any reparation, damages, or monetary loss due to the information herein, either directly or indirectly.

Respective authors own all copyrights not held by the publisher.

The information herein is offered for informational purposes solely, and is universal as so. The presentation of the information is without contract or any type of guarantee assurance.

The trademarks that are used are without any consent, and the publication of the trademark is without permission or backing by the trademark owner. All trademarks and brands within this book are for clarifying purposes only and are the owned by the owners themselves, not affiliated with this document.

TABLE OF CONTENTS

Introduction

Reiki practitioners believe the healing energy passes to the patient from the hands of the Reiki master.

Reiki is a treatment that is also characterized as palm healing or hands-on-body treatment, where a practitioner puts hands gently on or around the body of an individual to promote the treatment cycle of the individual.

Reiki combines "rei" (spiritual or supernatural) and "ki" (vital energy) in Japanese and Chinese word-characters. According to the National Center for Complementary and Integrative Health (NCCIH), one of the basic ideas held by those who practice Reiki is that this vital energy may be channeled to support the body's natural ability to heal itself.

However, there is no scientific evidence to support claims that so-called vital energy actually exists, nor is there any conclusive evidence that Reiki, according to the NCCIH, is useful for any health-related end. But despite the fact that Reiki has not proven to be effective in treating certain conditions of health, that doesn't mean it's a harmful practice.

"Reiki will do no good — the only thing it can achieve is nothing," said Ann Baldwin, a University of Arizona professor of physiology, and a qualified Reiki master or practitioner.

Reiki has been built into many health care settings in recent years, including hospitals, Baldwin told Live Science. According to the Center for Spirituality & Healing at the University of Minnesota (UMN), related evidence from some of the most clinically based research on Reiki indicate that this alternative treatment may play a role in minimizing distress and discomfort, promoting calm, increasing exhaustion and helping to alleviate depressive symptoms.

Reiki's Origin

The roots of Reiki are often disputed, although most accept that the technique goes back to the late nineteenth or early twentieth century, and the teachings of a Japanese monk named Mikao Usui. According to the Langone Medical Center of New York University, Usui bases his healing techniques on methods and philosophies drawn from several traditional Asian healing practices.

At the heart of Reiki is the principle — previously recognized in the Middle Ages of Western medicine and still used today in Eastern medicine — that sickness is induced by imbalances in the body 's essential energies and that fixing such imbalances facilitates regeneration, according to UMN's Spirituality & Regeneration Center.

Usui is claimed to have "rediscovered" this ancient idea of an inexhaustible reservoir of strength which can be harnessed to cure. A Reiki master (Usui was the first) can teach others to master this healing power, too, through a process called attunements. In 1937, following an extended period of Reiki training in Japan, a Japanese-American named HawayoTakata brought Reiki practice to the West when she returned to her native Hawaii, according to the International Center for Reiki Training.

How Reiki works

A patient typically lies down on a massage table during a Reiki therapy session. According to Baldwin, the Reiki practitioner places his or her hands over (or directly on top of) the patient's body in different positions, beginning at the head crown.

"The force of Reiki spreads from [his or her] hands from the practitioner to the individual lying on the bed," Baldwin said. However, she said, the precise process by which Reiki energy moves theoretically from one individual to another is unclear. And some Reiki masters claim to be able to treat patients without being near them anywhere-a practice known as "distance healing."

"No-one understands precisely how Reiki functions," said Baldwin. "One idea is that Reiki might be related to electromagnetic-type energy, and interact with the electromagnetic field of a person."

Another theory, according to UMN 's Center for Spirituality & Healing, is that Reiki promotes relaxation, which in turn lowers a patient's stress response and encourages healing. Nonetheless, according to the NCCIH, the general efficacy of Reiki is not well established in the medical literature.

Studies on Reiki

Most of the medical therapies are tested using what is known as a placebo-controlled double-blind study. Groups of patients in such studies are given either a real treatment or a fake treatment (such as sugar pill). According to Langone Medical Center, neither the trial subjects nor the experts themselves knew which patients got the actual thing, and which provided a so-called "sham diagnosis."

It is not possible to conduct a double-blind Reiki study, however, since the person administering the treatment will inevitably know whether he or she is administering the real thing or a sham treatment. Since Reiki cannot be evaluated by traditional means, it is often ignored out of hand by some inside the scientific profession.

But even those who in earnest look at Reiki studies have found no evidence that the practice is effective beyond the placebo effect. Among the largest studies on Reiki is a systematic review of all published research on Reiki, which appeared in the 2008 International Journal of Clinical Practices. The researchers concluded that most Reiki studies "suffered from methodological flaws like small sample size, inadequate study design and poor reporting" and "the evidence is insufficient to suggest that Reiki is an effective treatment for any condition."

However, this reality does not appear to discourage Reiki supporters such as Baldwin, who refer to other research demonstrating, for example, the efficacy of Reiki in reducing fear in hysterectomy women and decreasing discomfort in persons with chronic illness.

Reiki masters, Baldwin said, don't necessarily promise to cure their patients of whatever ails.

"For example, when Reiki is used on cancer patients it is not about healing the tumor. It is about making the patient more comfortable and reducing their pain and anxiety," Baldwin said. A recent study by University of Pennsylvania researchers found that Reiki actually serves that purpose for some cancer patients.

This book was written thematically first describing the various forms of Energy Healing, Reiki healing history, degrees of Reiki healing, chakras, healing powers of chakras etc. This book also sheds light on Aura's cleansing secrets and Reiki Yoga Meditation to boost your health, enhance your healing power and energy.

Chapter 1: Energy Healing- A Form of Complementary and Alternative Medicine

The use and application of complementary and alternative medicine (CAM) in today's health care is of great importance to patients, physicians, researchers and policy-makers. Of example, 42 percent of individuals in the U.S. reported having at least one CAM treatment, although less than 40 percent reported their usage to a practitioner.

At the same time as natural remedies or high-dose supplements, an estimated 15 million adults took prescription drugs in 1997, which put the risk of adverse reactions into play. Gross referrals to the CAM facilities exceed total appointments to all primary care doctors. CAM's out-of-pocket investment is valued at $27 billion, a sign that CAM is already a big business. Clinics, managed care systems and traditional professionals integrate CAM therapies into their services of health care. Health colleges, nursing schools, and pharmacy schools instruct their students about the Screen. The knowledge of CAM is openly publicized in various media such as newspapers, magazines, books, brochures and the Internet.

Friends talk to peers about the solutions to specific problems.

1.1 Health Care System's Quality and Effectiveness

Concerns about the use of CAM emerge at a time when traditional medical care services are being forced to unprecedentedly investigate the feasibility and effectiveness of health care in the United States. The Institute of Medicine's Crossing the Quality Chasm (IOM, 2001) provides sufficient proof in its delivery for underuse of successful treatment, overuse of moderately effective or ineffective treatment, and misuse of care, including preventable errors. Large variation in the rates of surgery and other care for medical problems among fairly identical demographics of various regional areas poses concerns regarding whether physicians and patients draw decisions.

It is critical for patients with symptoms or signs which decrease the quality of life or raise doubts about the lifespan. Around the same time, important yet compelling issues must be concerned with before decisions are made. So what's wrong really? And if I don't do anything, will it improve, get worse or stay the same? These are my diagnostic options, and what are the benefits and harms? What does he sound about the healing process? How definitely, by how much and for how long do I benefit from this? How likely am I to get hurt, for how long and how? People who do not have any illness and who wish to remain healthy raise similar questions. The strongest solutions to such concerns come from a base of scientific experience and can be more or less backed up with conclusive evidence relevant to the situation of the individual case. When these knowledge occurs and is successfully marshaled and communicated, the decisions and resulting treatment satisfy the purpose of being "reality-based."

Effective judgments rely heavier on technical knowledge of therapeutic choices and probabilities of outcome. The same symptoms can affect specific patients, more or less. We can respond differently to the experience of treatment itself, and expect different reactions to the benefits or harms, or both. Even though the evidence for the particular patient is so strong, there will still be some doubts about the outcomes. Risks considered worthless by some may be unacceptable to others. Benefits or disadvantages can more or less likely occur early or late, and the timing of the good and the bad affects patients' ability to make trade-offs between the two. If the opinions and expectations of individual patients are elicited and valued, decisions on diagnosis and prevention and subsequent care achieve the goal of being "patient-centered." Over the past decades, there has been a marked shift from relying on clinical expertise to increasingly focusing on more objective quantitative data among physicians who practice traditional medicine. These more systematic methods have been used more recently in CAM investigations. However, there are significant obstacles to the use of methods that have gained predominance in testing and advancing the knowledge base for traditional medical practitioners among the heterogeneous therapies involving CAM, in particular those that rely on variable practitioner approaches and the adaptation of therapies to individual patients.

Given the obvious disparities between conventional professional practice and CAM, maybe the most positive approach to reach common ground is to ask: what kind of experience do patients require to make successful decisions in health care, and how can this knowledge be continually verified and enhanced? The context for considering acceptable clinical and policy responses to the extensive use of CAM by the public is set out in this question.

In addition, this structure is based on a series of ethical commitments:

- Social commitment to public health
- Commitment to the safety of patients and the environment
- Respect for patient autonomy
- Acceptance of scientific pluralism, and
- Environment responsibility

1.2 CAM Defined

One of the challenges with each CAM research is to try to decide what is included in the CAM definition. Should CAM use the vitamins, foods and nutrition, behavioral medicine, exercise, and other therapies incorporated into mainstream medical systems? May CAM require yoga, shamanism or other therapies that would not be regarded as health-care procedures? The explanations for classifying modalities as "CAM treatments" are not only science but also "financial, social, and metaphysical" (Jonas, 2002).

Relaxation methods, herbs, chiropractic, and massage therapy are among the most widely used and well-known treatments that are recognized as CAM throughout the United States (Eisenberg et al. 1998). Some state the chiropractic license, acupuncture, and massage therapy. Naturaluropathy and Homeopathy are approved for fewer states. Many other treatments and procedures are considered unlicensed activities, and generally these interventions and modalities are subject to little to no specific legislation. The New York State Office for Regulatory Reform and CAM listed more than 100 procedures, practices, and programs which could be called CAM.

The literature finds a lack of continuity in describing what's included in CAM. CAM is defined as "a culture of diverse structures, methods and products of medical and health care not widely accepted as part of mainstream medicine" (NCCAM, 2002). Others would argue, however, that if it has been proved safe and successful, and is used in traditional practice, a treatment does not cease to be a CAM treatment. "Just because a herbal cure comes to be used by doctors does not mean that herbalists cease to practice, or that the practice of one is like that of the other" (Hufford, 2002).

CAM's succinct meanings include one by Ernst et al. (1995), who wrote that CAM is a' diagnosis, cure and/or prevention that complements traditional medicine by adding to a larger culture, addressing a need not provided by orthodox medicine, or diversifying the philosophical framework of medicine.' Gevitz (1988) proposes that CAM include "those practices that are not accepted as being correct, correct or appropriate or that do not conform to the beliefs or standards of the dominant group of medical practitioners in a society."

Due to the lack of a clear concept of CAM, others have tried to explain the situation by suggesting classification schemes which can be used to organize the sector. Several of the grouping structures most widely used, established by NCCAM (2000), divides CAM modalities into five categories:

• Holistic medical approaches,
• Mind-body strategies,
• Scientifically based treatments,
• Psychological and body-related methods and
• Energy therapy

Complementary and complementary medicine (CAM) technologies and uses are comprised of many specific areas. However, several parts of a field can overlap with other pieces of field. E.g., acupuncture is often utilized in standard medicine. Adults about 38 percent and children 12 percent in the United States use CAM. Many of the examples given below are CAM:

1.3 Conventional Medical Systems

This area encompasses the more conventional and accepted therapeutic approaches, like homeopathy, acupuncture, and Oriental therapy. Such treatments are in practice for decades around the world. Traditional or conventional supplementary medicinal products might include the following:

• Ayurveda

• Acupuncture

• Naturopathy

• Homeopathy

• Oriental or Chinese medicine

Mind-Body Interventions

Since the health care system early history, health care has utilized touch as a form of healing. Touch healing is an idea based that all the body areas in one body region can be affected by disease or damage. Body treatment styles include Massage, body activity exercises, Tai Chi, and Yoga.

External Energy-Body-based Approaches

Many people assume a person's health is directly influenced by external energy coming from other sources or objects. Examples of therapy of external energy include electromagnetic, Reiki, and Qigong therapy.

Mind and Senses

Medicine normal or traditional one recognizes the strength of the bond between the mind and the body. It is shown by studies that people who are physically and emotionally healthy tend to cure rapidly compared to people who are physically and emotionally ill. Therapies that use mind can involve sleep, biofeedback, and hypnosis.

Many people argue that senses such as touch, hearing, sight, taste, and smell can all influence health overall. Examples of sensory therapies include painting, music, dance, guided, and visualization imaging.

1.4 Types of Energy Healing

Research has shown that if people have strong emotional and mental well-being, they also get better and heal faster. Energy healing is a conventional healing method that restores energy balance and the flow of energy through the body, mind and soul. Specifically this approach deals with the physical, mental and spiritual aspects of wellness. This is commonly used to treat different medical disorders, especially psychiatric illnesses.

This describes the illness triggered by the disruption in the supply of energy to the body. It is assumed that when the energy flow is fixed the individual gets healed automatically. There are numerous forms of healing-energy therapies that function differently to heal a person. The most important forms of techniques for healing energy are:

Theta Healing

This approach focuses on meditation and prayer for the actual healing process, depending on God / Source. As the practitioner Donald Simon has described, the practitioner goes into a (deep meditative) theta brain wave state, asks God (or Source) for support, and then observes the healing.

Theta Healing believes the immediate rendering of physical and emotional changes is possible.

Aromatherapy

Aromatherapy is where fragrances such as these are inhaled to bring back balance between mind, body and soul. The oils are extracted from certain flowers, trees, and herbs to produce effective fragrances.

Hypnosis

Hypnosis happens when the patient is reaching a hypnotic state. A hypnotic state is a modified mode of consciousness which makes the patient more inclined towards suggestive forces. Usually used to alter unhealthy habits, heal a phobia, and reduce pain.

Detoxification

It works by having your body cleaned. Toxins are usually processed through the body. A strict diet must be followed for a specified period of time to allow ample time for the body to properly eliminate all the toxins from its bloodstream.

Massage and Reflexology

Both are now seen as more traditional medical treatments, though acupuncture and reflexology were previously considered complementary therapies. Both can bring tremendous benefits for the health, especially when used to manage painful muscles. Reflexology operates on the premise that there are pressure points in the feet that relate to the various parts of the body, and that working with these pressure points will help to ease problems in the linked body regions.

Pranic Healing

Pranic Healing is about utilizing the body's life force to restore the body's energies. Such treatment particularly works on the energy or aura of a person's body. During this procedure, energy is used to cleanse the contaminants from the body, thereby enhancing the internal recovery cycle.

Crystal Healing

Cristal curing stones and crystals are used during this healing process to remove impurities from the body. These stones and crystals work differently on the body and cope with various types of physical, emotional, and spiritual issues. We repel the poisonous energies of the organism, which disturbs both physical and mental health.

Quantum Healing

Quantum healing therapy is focused upon the theory of resonance and entertainment. Quantum Touch sets out specific emphasis on the patient's use of breath to improve the procedure. Practitioners create their own energies and bring the customer's energies to a higher (healthier) level.

Breathing and visualizing the flow of energy escalates the level of energy in the body. Quantum Healing stresses not just the spiritual dimension but also the positive impact on the immune system.

Qigong

Qigong therapy is used to recover the lost balance in the body. With some 4,000 years of practice, Qigong consists of coordinated body movements coupled with relaxation, and meditation to encourage spirituality and wellbeing. The therapy has its origins in Chinese medicine and is believed to regulate the good energies needed by the body to remain alive.

Acupuncture / Acupressure

Such two therapies are part of an ancient and nuanced body-centered therapy system focused on a non-Western pattern, with a negligible distinction in their titles. We are working to balance chi / ki / qi as it traverses the body's meridian network.

Chakra Healing

Chakra healing is a general term for the energy of healing which works via the chakra system. The chakras are a pillar of our power grid. There are so many ways to heal energy through any sort of chakra work. Chakra Therapy has more than 500 down to earth tasks and techniques that can be used to control, develop and heal your own chakras.

Emotional Freedom Techniques (EFT)

EFT, or Emotional Freedom Techniques, is one of the easily taught, meridian-based forms of energy cure. This includes acupuncture with a mind-body treatment, without needles.

Energy-focused Bodywork

The body is often ignored, as part of the energy system. Nevertheless, all is energy and this implies that the body is also energy. Every bodywork (massage) has an effect on your strength but it is deliberate in some ways. Lomi lomi, Trager, shiatsu, and cranio-sacral therapy are examples of those that deliberately use subtle force.

Healing Touch (HT)

This originated from the US registered nursing culture in the 1980s. There are many HT professionals in the

U.S., and the well-developed HT Community holds them in high regard.

Intuitive Healing

Intuitive Healing is a broad concept which can refer to any healing act or method which uses intuition to help direct the process of healing or treatment. While the word is typically used for energy healers and other holistic healers, it could be used just as accurately by many traditional medical practitioners. A doctor may practice evidence-based medicine, but this still does not rule out the use of intuition in a judgmental way.

Polarity Therapy

Polarity therapy is based on the concept of energetic attraction, repulsion and neutrality. Dr. Randolph Stone, DO, DC, ND (1890–1981) developed it. Like other forms of energy research, Polarity Therapy aims to identify blockages, release energy into normal flow patterns, and maintain the bioenergetic environment in an open, versatile state. PT can involve diet , exercise, and self-consciousness, as well as dependence on energy for bodywork.

Restorative Touch

Restorative Contact is a specific and powerful energy therapy approach that works on a resonance paradigm to "support health, regeneration, and spiritual growth." Using strict qualification and licensing requirements, professionals are extremely trained and held to high expectations.

Shamanic Healing

Shamanic healers take energy from the divine world, invoking supernatural helps such as influential animals or other divine powers. Shamanic practice is used to treat a range of mental and physical illnesses.

Spiritual Healing

Spiritual Healing is closely associated with energy healing.

Magnetic Pulse

For complementary treatment counseling is widely used. This therapy utilizes magnets. This approach works on the premise that electromagnetic fields can help to rebalance body energy levels.

Counseling

Counseling and other psychotherapy methods are meant to change ways of thinking and can help cure mental illnesses. In stress, depression, mental problems, and addictions, these techniques used.

Sound Healing

Sound Healing works by listening to music or sounds that calm the body's vibrations and elevate them to the desirable optimum healing state.

Hydrotherapy

Uses water to manage illnesses and pathogens, to prevent them. It contains numerous water uses including saunas, steam baths, salt rubs, immersion pools and colonic irrigation.

Yoga

Yoga can help balance body and mind, and enhance muscle function, flexibility, strength.

Psychic Healing

Spiritual or psychological therapy uses therapeutic rituals. Prayers, incantations, and special rituals of healing come under this category.

Color Healing

Colors connect with different parts of the body. It is assumed that visualizing the right color coupled with regular exposure to that color, wearing clothes of that color and consuming foods of that color will improve the healing process.

1.5 Reiki Healing

Reiki is probably the most well recognized method of energy therapy, and simple to understand and practice. It is an alternative form of therapy which is commonly called energy healing. This originated in late 1800s in Japan, and is claimed to entail fundamental energy transmutation from the hands of the practitioner to their recipient.

In different forms for centuries, there has been the utilization of Energy healing. Advocates say around the body, work together of the energy fields.

Reiki is surrounded by some debate, as it is impossible to show its validity through experimental methods. However, a lot of people say about the working of Reiki who receives it, and it is growing in popularity. A search by Google yield results of more than 68,900,000.

A survey in 2007 shows that at least once in the previous year adults (1.2 million) in the United States (U.S.) tried Reiki therapy or therapy similar to it. More than sixty hospitals are thought to be offering patients Reiki services.

Reiki Facts

Some Reiki points are here. More detail is provided in this topic.

The energy therapy form is Reiki.

In some circles despite skepticism, in popularity, it is growing.

It involves energy transfer by hands laying.

Reiki's supporters believe that many emotional states and conditions can be treated by it.

Pain can be slightly relieved by reiki according to some studies, but disease treatment is not proven in studies mostly.

Reiki is offered by some hospitals in Europe and America, but usually, it is not included in insurance

What is in actual Reiki?

The energy is transferred by the practitioner in Reiki by placing his hands on the victim or over him. The "mysterious aura, magical symbol is meant by word Reiki." This word is a Japanese word in which "Rei" means universal and "ki" means life energy. Reiki is one type of calming force. Energy healing is targeting all fields of energy all over the body. In the body, the Energy can stagnate where physical damage there is, or probably emotional distress, according to practitioners. Those blocks of energy can results in illness in time. Similar to acupuncture or acupressure, the energy flow, and to remove blocks are mainly aimed by energy medicine. Improving the energy flow through the body, claim practitioners, can result in enabling relaxing, pain reduction, speed healing, and decrease different symptoms of the disease. Reiki's been there for millennia. Its modern type was first created by a Buddhist (Japanese) in 1922 named Mikao Usui, in his lifetime who supposedly taught more than 2,000 people the technique of Reiki. Throughout the 1940s the trend expanded to the United States by Honolulu, and in the 1980s to Europe. It is referred commonly as healing the palm, or healing by hand.

A session of Reiki

In a peaceful environment, it is best held but it can also be done anywhere. On a convenient chair, a patient sits or lays on a comfortably dressed bed. Depending on the patient's choice music is there.

For between 2 and 5 mins, the practitioner lightly places his hands on specific areas like the head, torso, and limbs using various hand forms. The hands, on over twenty different body areas, can be placed.

If there is serious damage, such as fire burn, then the hands should be placed right above the bite.

The practitioner while lightly holds his hands or above the body, there is energy transfer. The practicer hands can be wet and tingling at this period. Increasing hand location is retained until the energy flow stoppage is not confirmed by the practitioner.

When there is a feeling of energy or some heat reduction in the hands of practitioners, they may withdraw them and will position them on a different part.

Some Techniques of Reiki

Following names the technique involved usually:

- Beaming
- Centering
- Clearing
- Infusing
- harmful energies extraction
- smoothing aura and raking it

Few Reiki practitioners are going to use healing wands of chakra and crystals as they see that they can make healing possible or protect from negative energies, a home.

But the chair of the United Kingdom's Reiki Federation Annie Harrington told the Medical News:

"Reiki does not depend on any other tools other than practitioners. As a general rule, we don't use powders, crystals, or wands. Reiki healing one benefit is distance healing (several miles Reiki can be sent), crystals will be used by many practitioners to help with the vibrations of energy.

The sessions can be of 15-90 mins. The sessions will change according to client needs. Some customers prefer one session only while others prefer more sessions for solving a specific issue.

Reiki's Health Benefits

The effects of health are arbitrated by the channeling of universal energy qi, and pronounced as "chi," according to practitioners. This is called "prana," in India which is the similar energy that is involved in the exercise of tai chi. It's the energy of life-force that some belief surrounds us all. There is a theory that this force permeates the body. Experts of Reiki pointed out that during current analytical methods will not quantify this force, it was sensed by those who tuned in it. Reiki claims to help relax, support in the natural process of healing of the body, and develop spiritual, mental, and emotional well-being. It's said also in deep relaxation induction, help people in difficulties management, alleviate emotional pressure, and enhance overall wellness. People describe Reiki as "intense relaxation", who receives it usually. Conditions Reiki was used in helping with the treatment include:

- heart disease
- cancer
- depression
- neurodegenerative disorders
- anxiety
- chronic pain
- fatigue syndromes
- Crohn's disease
- autism
- infertility

According to the patients of Minnesota University who have been under a session of Reiki may say about:

"They feel refreshed and look like they are thinking clearly."

"They think they fell asleep."

"They cannot believe how much hot the hands are!"

"About feeling more relaxed as compared to massage relaxation."

"About headache is not there now."

Patients with cancer who have undergone Reiki say about feeling better afterward. That could be because it is helping them to relax. According to the UK Cancer Research, another reason may be the therapist with them will spend time and touch them. This affects patients who could be overloaded with intrusive treatment, anxiety, and pain. Individuals report varying experiences. Many claim the hands of the practitioner are becoming warmer, some mention the cooling hand's feelings and some feel the waves pulsating. The common reports mostly are of deep relaxation and stress relief.

Individuals report varying experiences. Many claim the hands of the practitioner are becoming warmer, some mention the cooling hands and some people feel the waves pulsating. The most common reports are of stress relief and deep relaxation. Individuals report varying experiences. Many claim the hands of the practitioner are becoming warmer, some mention the cooling hands and some people feel the waves pulsating. The most common reports are of stress relief and deep relaxation.

How can you become a Reiki Practitioner?

To join the Reiki class, or "attunement method," no previous preparation, knowledge, or expertise is required. In this phase, the instructor is claimed as a "strong divine force," to transmit the energies of attunement and healing methods through the pupil.

Training of Reiki varies, but students mostly learn about the following:

Body energies

• Working with the energy of healing

Tuning preparation includes 2-3 day fasting, meditation, nature focusing, and release of negative emotions. Three Mastery levels are there. Many that achieve the stage of "Master" will instruct many, and they can apparently heal them from distance, similar to a prayer type.

Evidence on Reiki's healing power

Although Reiki is increasing in importance there are still concerns. Reiki promises to promote relaxing, rising discomfort, speed recovery, and relieve other effects, but limited scientific results support any concrete benefits of health. Without scientific proof, it usually faces criticism to cure illnesses. Many have described their assertions as a fraud.

Critics claim about its face flying in the current nature's laws understanding. Advocates reply that, in a quantitative analysis, the effects of health and decreased tension are possible but usually hard to quantify.

Scientists notice that there is a shortage of high-quality studies into its efficacy. No research yet has proven it to be far more successful than placebo, they add.

A 2008 literature review concluded about insufficient evidence there in Reiki's support of being a productive treatment for all the conditions, and also that value of it is unproven remained.

In 2015, Cochrane published a study review on Reiki and depression and anxiety treatment. The conclusion by investigators was about "less evidence were there about Reiki usefulness to people over the age of 16 with depression or anxiety or both." The few studies that were completed were mostly of low quality, having sample sizes small, no control group, and peer review.

Meanwhile, BMC Nephrology published research has talked about that it might be worthwhile to allow patients of dialysis, for example, for having benefit from the "touch of healing," especially if freely offered by volunteers. The reduction in pain might be slight only, but non-traumatic it is and no harm it does and let the patients feel that they are themselves "doing something" to relieve their pain.

To MNT recently Annie Harrington told that the Reiki Federation of U.K. has currently "many documents cataloging about many trials of research." Perhaps these findings, studied by the CNHC (Complementary and Natural Healthcare Council) and federation of the United Kingdom will help in bringing Reiki in the mainstream even further.

Is harmful Reiki is?

The United States NCCIH (National Center for Complementary and Integrative Health) states that Reiki "was not shown clearly in useful for any of the purpose health-related." However, it was added by them that this doesn't show any effects that can be harmful.

The biggest issue seems that people having serious issues of health may prefer Reiki and holistic treatments like these rather than rigorously validated conventional medicine. Nevertheless, it is known to be dangerous unless used with other therapies.

Indeed, contact alone, with universal energy or without it seems to have a variety of advantages, from increasing trust to improving general well-being.

The Reiki cure is not only designed to heal the diseases but also to correct the mind by virtue of a spiritual ability sent from God. It keeps the body safe, and helps a person enjoy a worry-free life. Helping them understand the last orders of Emperor Meiji along with chanting morning and evening the 5 admonitions are important when teaching Reiki healing to people. The five warnings are:

• Don't get angry today

• Don't be grievous
• Show your gratitude
• Be vigilant in your company
• Be kind to others

In the next chapters we will explore in detail Reiki therapy, its past and roots, Reiki chakras and aura, Reiki stages and Reiki attunement along with the benefits and applications of this incredible healing technique.

Chapter 2: History of Reiki Healing

Several attempts have been made to understand the origins of Reiki, but sadly, in the past, many of them have been mostly focused on speculation and an effort to endorse a specific style of Reiki and lacked precise details during most.

At the present, empirical and credible knowledge regarding the history of Reiki is continuously changing, when more and more fresh research is coming to light from Japan. There is Western interpretation of events opposite Japanese version of events. However, to avoid getting caught up in the right and wrong interpretations of its history, we have to note that this energy is all about healing and love and that we just have to remain open-minded in order to remain true to the energy.

The following is a comprehensive history of Reiki, drawn from evidence-based facts and knowledge based on written documents and interviews with those close to its creation and evolution:

2.1 Usui Reiki Healing System

Usui Reiki's history begins with a glance at the inscription on the memorial stone. It was erected in 1927 in Tokyo, Japan, in honor of the father of the Usui Reiki Healing Method, Mikao Usui Sensei.

The inscription was written on the Usui Memorial by Juzaburo Ushida, a Shihan (teacher) who had been trained by Usui Sensei, He was also willing to practice Reiki to perform almost the same as Usui did. He also replaced Usui Sensei as president of the Ryoho Gakkai Usui Reiki (Usui Reiki Healing System Society).

He started a new way of improving the world of body and spirit. REIKI was based on this system. Hearing the news, people who wanted to know the remedy at once and get the cure gathered from everywhere.

Dr Mikao Usui and his Ancestors (1865 – 1926)

Usui-Sensei's popular name was Mikao, whilst his pen name was Gyohan. He hailed from village Taniai. Tsunetane Chiba was one of its forefathers. Tsunetane Chiba had remained very active as a military commander and exhibited excellent skills. During the time between the Heian Era and the Kamakura Time (1180–1230), he showed certain outstanding skills.

Usui's Discovery of Reiki Healing

He was eager to research and focused diligently on his studies. He traveled to China and Europe to obtain advanced education as he grew older. His education covered religion, medicine, and psychology as well as divination arts. Asians also treated the art of divination as a worthy ability. He was also affiliated with the Rei Jyutuu Ka, a philosophical group devoted to psychological ability building. He served many roles, including civil servant, journalist, and company executive, and helped in rehabilitating the inmates. Eventually he was the Director of Shinpei Goto, Head of Department of Health and Welfare. Shinpei Goto was subsequently elected as Tokyo's mayor. Usui Sensei experiences through this work helped him turn into a successful businessman, too.

The intensity and nature of his encounters influenced him to concentrate his focus on discovering the meaning of life. Across the idea of a specific consciousness state during his journey he came, which, if learned and gained, wouldn't only offer an awareness of the nature of one's life, but also guides one in its furtherance. This specific state is called An-shin Ritus-mei (pronounced as may be on sheen dit sue).). One's still at ease in this unique condition, whatever occurs in the outside world. This quiet place completes one's life meaning. The unique features of this state is that it sustains itself without any work from the individual; the sense of peace in turn grows naturally from inside and becomes a sort of self-awareness. Usui Sensei recognized the notion on an abstract basis and committed his life trying to follow it; this was seen as a significant step in Usui Sensei's spiritual journey. He pointed out that one way to Anshin Ritsu-mei is via practicing of the Zazen way of meditation. And he met a Zen instructor who welcomed him as a pupil very openly and began teaching him Zazen practice. After 3 years of service, he didn't succeed and looked for more guidance. The tutor told him about a more extreme form, making it mandatory for the student to make his life in Anshin Ritsu-mei's attainment. So with that inside his mind, he prepared for the worst outcome and in Feb of 1922, he made his way to Kurama Yama, a mountain towards the north of the city of Kyoto. He was going there fasting and meditating until he had gone over to the other world. It should be remembered that he did not intend to find a healing process but instead was trying to understand that unique spiritual condition.

However, there is a tiny waterfall somewhere on Kurama Yama which even to this day is a popular meditation site. This exercise involves standing beneath the waterfall letting the water strike the head, a practice being said to stimulate the crown chakra. It is suggested by Japanese Reiki Masters that Usui Sensei could have used this method in his work. He became weaker and frailer as time passed. On 21st March at midnight, a blinding light unexpectedly reached his mind from above his head, and he thought he had been hit by lightning; this resulted in him losing his consciousness. As morning came, he woke up and found that although through his fasting he felt extremely tired, he now was overflowing with a very pleasant state of health that he hadn't felt before; a mystical type of powerful spiritual energy had drained his normal self and substituted it with an astoundingly fresh level of perception. He regarded himself as the strength and awareness of the Cosmos, and that he obtained the exceptional condition of liberation he desired as a reward. This recognition has made him exceptionally satisfied. As that occurred, he was overflowing with happiness, and went downhill to the base of the mountain to inform his Zen teacher of his wonderful fortune. He accidentally tipped on a rock and fell. And just like anyone, he placed his hands on the leg, which was hurt. As he did so, energy that heals began to flow from his very hands. The agony in his foot had gone away, and then and there the ankle was healed. That made Usui Sensei shocked. He knew that, besides the life changing incident he had experienced, he was also given the power of healing. He even remembered his purpose in life; becoming a healer, and educating others. In the April of 1922, he shifted to Tokyo and began a healing community, called Usuii Reiki Ryoho Gakkaii (Usui Reiki Healing Process Society). He even founded a Reiki Harajuku center in Aoyama city, Tokyo. Over there he conducted workshops and provided recovery programs. At first Usui sensei only had his healing prowess. With the passage of time he established his own way of doing Reiki. Any of such developments come after the 1923 Great Kanto tsunami and earthquake, which caused major destruction in Tokyo, killing and wounding thousands. Because too many citizens required support, Usui Sensei thought he should transfer these talents over to others to make them become teachers and thereby aid the injured in these desperate and troubling circumstances. During this period he studied all of his practitioner's methods, like Gassho, Byosen screening, Reijiho, Seishin-to-iitsu, Gyoshii-ho, etc. He also created a systematic attunement system, or Reiju kaii, making it easy for many to learn Reiki, and ultimately helping them become teachers. The technique he used earlier to flow the Reiki ability was literally holding the hands of the patient but it took a large amount of time. The Reiju kai made it much faster for Reiki to move skill. He created the symbols for Reiki too. He'd had three Reiki symbols during the early period. They are 3 indications that we earn during Reiki II in today's environment where he called by the name of Okuden. Around the point he didn't have a Master symbol ring. This crucial argument was mentioned by someone of the Gakka by the name of Hiroshi, as he had conversations with many of the Gakkai higherups and with some of the Shinpiden. Arjava Petter Sensei, well aquainted with the Gakkai's Shinpiden teachers and its president, also confirmed this very fact. These very sources often say Usui Sensei had given each student many tunings, not just a single set. The goal of doing this attunement regularly with the student was so this experience continually enhanced and reinforced one's capacity to manipulate Reiki energy, allowing the energy funneled to be more robust and capable of curing a broader range of situations, curing more effectively and with a shorter period. The belief of Usui Sensei stated that the nature and potency of Reiki energies present in the world is not constrained. Consequently, an important goal for both pupils was to continuously strive to better the efficiency and potency of Reiki energies that can be channeled.

Degrees of Usui Reiki Healing

In its simpler form, he named his healing tactic ShinShin KaiZen Usuii Reiki RyoHo (Usui Reiki Mind and Body Improvement Treatment Method), or Usui Reikii Ryoho (Usuii Reiki method of healing).

Shoden–First Degree

His first degree had the name Shoden (meaning First Degree) and was distributed into four stages:

- Loku-Tou
- Go-Tou
- Yon-Tou
- San-Tou

Once Takata Sensei instructed this phase she mixed all 4 levels into a single phase, which is referred to as

Reiki Stage I in the West. That is most probably the reason she did 4 Level I settings.

Okuden the Inner Teaching-Second Degree

Okuden (Inner Teaching) preceded Shoden, had 2 stages: Okuden-Zen-ki (1st part) and and the 2nd part was Okuden-Koe-ki.

Shinpiden (Mystery Teaching)

The corresponding degree was by the name of Shinpiden (Teaching of Mystery), this is referred to as a Masters degree by most Western Reikis. Shinpiden's degree consists of Shihan (venerable teacher) and ShihanKaku (assistant teacher),

Reikki was demanded so much that Usui Sensei had to enlarge his practice, and he made a larher one in 1925 in Nakano city, Tokyo. His fame as a powerful healer extended across Japan, expanding his clinic and starting to send Reiki energy to a vast number of people. He started traveling so he was able to teach more people and hand out treatment to people who were ailing. He instructed approximately 2,000 pupils directly in his journeys through Japan and established twenty Shihan, each possessing the same interpretation of Reiki, approving of teaching and offering Reiju the same manner as Usui sensei.

Major Emphasis of Usui-Sensei in Reiki Healing

Usui-Sensei emphasized that 'This is certainly a secret way of delivering wealth, and indeed a divine cure for curing all manner of diseases,' through which he made his teaching purpose clear and specific. He tried to make his teaching approach as simple and straightforward as possible, so there is nothing complicated to think about. Each time you develop a pure and sound mind; sit in a still mode. Then raise your hands to fast and sing morning and evening, and that is the only meaning for your everyday life. You have to make the best of it. Therefore the Reiki cure can be spread to everyone very quickly.

The life process is very unpredictable in these days, and the thoughts of the people are often apt for change. If we could only distribute the Reiki remedy everywhere, we feel sure that preventing citizens from disordering their sense of confidence will be quite helpful. In terms of harm to people, this never does anything but brings with it benefits of treating long-term disease, chronic illness and bad habit.

2.2 Dr. Chujiro Hayashi (1878–1940)

Before death, Usui Sensei requested Chujiiro Hayashi Sensei to establish a Reiki clinic by himself and, on the basis of him being a former Navy medical practitioner, to expand and develop Reiki Ryoho. The Hayashi Sensei, inspired by this wish, founded a clinic and school named Hayashi Reiki Kenkyukai. At his home in Japan, he maintained careful accounts documenting all diseases and disorders of his patients. He even recorded which hand positions were optimal for which disorder. Looking at these observations, he established the Reiki Ryoho Shinshin (Reiki Instructions for Healing Techniques). This guide to healing was in a class pamphlet he provided to his pupils. If and only if he found it challenging and extremely difficult to use Byosen scanning to find the optimum manual hand positions to practice, the practitioner could turn to the use of handbook. Most of his pupils had their Reiki trainings in his clinic as a pay for jobs. Hayashi Sensei has also altered the technique Reiki was taught initially. Instead of getting the client sitting in a seat and receiving treatment from one person as Usui did in his treatment method, Hayashi Sensei made the patient lie flat on a table. The individual was then handled by several clinicians at once. Hayashi Sensei has also created a more improved system for Reiju giving.

Dr Hayashi had taught about 14 students at the time of his death to become Reiki Masters. One such individual was Ms. Hawayo Takata, a Japanese-American woman who went to Dr. Hayashi initially to treat Reiki. Due to Mrs.Takata Reiki came to be recognized in the West.

2.3 Mrs. Hawayo Takata (1900-1980)

Mrs. Hawayo Takatas date of birth was 24 December 1900, she was born on Kauai island, Hawaii. Her parents had been refugees from japan, and her dad had worked in cane sugar fields. She was infected with a kidney, gallstones, appendicitis and asthma after her visit to a doctor with a lengthy and disabling disease. She had been told to be ready for surgery but instead wanted to attend the Hayashi Sensei clinic. Mrs. Takata was not acquainted with the art of Reiki and was struck by the fact that the Reiki practitioners' care at the clinic strongly mirrored that of the doctor at her hospital. Soon she started undertaking therapies. Two Reiki therapists treat her work. Their hands produced such powerful heat, she said, she thought some sort of special equipment was being used. Viewing the wide sleeves worn by one of the Japanese traditional kimono, she felt she would find the hidden location of disguise. She scared the doctor one day by pulling his sleeves, but found nothing. After she described what she did, he started laughing, and then informed her how reiki works. Mrs. Takata gradually strengthened and recovered fully in 4 months. As for herself, she has decided to learn more about Reiki. In 1936, Dr Hayashi awarded her First Degree Reiki. She then served with him one year and obtained Second Reiki degree. In the year 1937, Mrs. Takata moved to Hawaii, accompanied shortly after by Hayashi Sensei, who came to aid her in establishing a Reiki centre. In February of 1938, he Hayashi Sensei began Hawayo Takata as Master of Reiki. In Hawaii, Takata Sensei performed Reiki making many clinics, one of them was situated in Big Island, Hilo. She provided therapies and educated students until Reiki II. Afterwards, she became a famous healer then travelled to the mainland of the United States and many areas around the world to educate and provide therapies. He was a good healer who had credited her results on any client to having done a large amount of

Reiki. She will sometimes perform quite few procedures, each lasting for hours. She handled challenging and complex cases every day for many months, till her clients were healed. They often asked members of family of a customer to assist in this phase so they could also be able to supply the person in Reiki. Takata Senseis style of conducting and studying Reiki was special varied greatly from the way Hayashi Sensei or Usui Sensei studied and exercised.

John Harvey Gray was among Takata Sensei's most admired pupils, and in addition she indicated that he would be one of 3 Reiki Masters to take out her study after her retirement. He suggested in a book that he wrote that Takata Sensei had modified the procedure she performed Reiki as the Japanese form was so complex to learn, so it should be impossible for the Western people to grasp. She streamlined the program for this reason. It included developing her very own hand placement technique, which she designated as the base care. It was placing eight hands on the shoulders, the belly and the head. If the customer needed them she even offered those additional back places. This differed markedly from the way Hayashi Sensei and Usui Sensei worked by educating Byosen scanning as a way to identify the best places for hand-held treatment of patients. They said that Byosen scanning was a very effective practice method for a pupil to learn continuously following the phase of having several Reijus. Except, this method was never taught by Takata Sensei. She did not therefore demonstrate some of the other various techniques used by Hayashi Sensei and Usuii Sensei, like gasho, Reiji-ho, Kenyoku, Gyoshi-ho, Koki-ho, etc. She also had a different method of attunement for each Reiki stage, trained her pupils that the attunement reinforced the symbols, and she taught her Master students a symbol. In her program the Master symbol was used to provide attunements, additionaly it could even be used during sessions of Reiki for healing purposes. Takata didn't allow her pupils to get as many settings as possible as Hayashi Sensei and Usui Sensei taught, but preached that I was enough for Reiki to have only a single set of 4 settings. Similarly, she taught them to have 2 or less tunings for Reiki II, and just one would suffice for Master level. The simplified approach taught by Takata Sensei has been effective and proven useful for both her students and clients. From the details presented, it can easily be concluded that Usui Reiki Ryoho's Takata Sensei is a significant innovator. A crucial thing to note is; if not for Takata Sensei, the art of Reiki would be unknown and wouldn't been done by citizens anywhere in the world including Japan, it would have remained totally obscure. The reason is that the U.S. wanted Japan to surrender unconditionally during World War II. That placed the U.S. having a lot of control over Japan. Any of the constraints that the US put is that anyone who performed any sort of healing had to possess a certificate. Many of the healing societies got approved but Usui Reiki Ryoho Gakkai determined that they didn't want a government authority to oversee them and instead decided to move under the ragar. They agreed the members would not reveal any information about Reiki except to the members. It made thinking of Reiki in Japan difficult for everyone, even the locals. In addition, membership gradually reduced, as new members were challenged to join. Since Takata Sensei had learned the art of Reiki in Japan before World War II after which she to Hawaii and started practicing Reiki, she was stopping Reiki from becoming a forgotten art. She was a wonderful instructor and champion, and she conducted Reiki classes in Honolulu and around the coasts of the USA. By the time she died she had attuned 22 total Reiki Masters. She died December 11, 1980.Since then, these Reiki Masters have started to instruct, and the Reiki Tradition is spreading more and through. Reiki is the fastest-growing complementary therapy that is practiced today in the world and this truth speaks volumes about this outstanding healing energy method.

2.4 The Evolution of Reiki

The possibilities Reiki has to give are limitless. As Hayashi Sensei, Usui Sensei and Takata Sensei had explained, Reiki is an art that is meant to be improved. It refers to the methods used to do Reiki but this often relates to the soothing energy level. The Reiki energy emerges from a limitless source, and as a result, no matter how perfected and sophisticated healing energy has been, only a limited amount of the possible healing energy available can be channeled. Increasing the consistency, efficacy and gain of one's healing energies is often important. Procedure that involves Attunements, Placements, and Ignitions aims to achieve the ideal condition. And Usui Sensei also alluded to this by saying he was not at the top of Reiki's healing system, but rather one level down.

CHAPTER 3: Applications and Benefits of Reiki Healing for the Beginners

In 1922, Mikao Usui, a Japanese Buddhist, founded Reiki therapy or Reiki Healing as explained in the previous part. This is an alternate cure process.

Reiki is a technique described as palm healing or hands-on-body treatment, in which a practitioner very carefully puts hands on or around a patient's body to facilitate the patient's healing process.

This is a Japanese therapeutic method used for strengthening the body's natural healing strength, relieving tension and relaxation. The "laying on hands" is performed to move the unseen "life-force-energy" that passes between us to a patient. If a person's "life-force-energy" is low, so they are more likely to get sick or feel discomfort, while if life-force-energy is strong, they are more likely to be healthy and secure.

Reiki is a blend of "rei" (spiritual or supernatural) and "ki" (vital energy) Japanese and Chinese word-characters. NCCIH, which is an abbreviation for The National Center for Complementary and Integrative Health, says that one of the basic concepts retained by Reiki practitioners is that this essential energy can be channeled to help the natural healing capacity of the body itself.

3.1 Reiki-An Intelligent Energy

Reiki is an intelligent energy which knows how to reach the environment where healing needs to take place. Reiki knows how to restore harmony back to where it got lost. It is necessary for a practitioner to realize that as a practitioner he should not be administering a Reiki treatment. Reiki should deliver the results you need, not by what you are trying to coerce or forcefully achieve. It is essential to note in the above that it is the task as a physician to pass this life force into the recipients' bodies, thus focusing on specific locations. And the job is not to control what Reiki does. Reiki should flow according to the maximum advantage of the receiver. Reiki flows for the sole purpose of restoring harmony and healing. It's also important to note that a practitioner should attempt to cure the problem's cause, not the symptoms. That should be the goal and should remain focused whenever a Reiki healing session is conducted by a practitioner For example, imagine a person who has back pain is looking for a Reiki healing session.

Was it more important to focus on pain relief, or fixing the root cause of the pain? Remember always removing the trigger takes the impact away. Symptoms may not disappear instantly, it's important that someone who seeks Reiki understands that. One should not be intimidated however, and must start holding Reiki classes. Time is a healer and while you are getting handled with Reiki healing you have to be well conscious of this reality. It calms and reduces stress, promoting healing in turn. And this approach has plenty. Practitioners use "laying on hands," mantras, and prayers to clear the energies of the body and improve the flow of life-force energies to flush out the mental and emotional contaminants that compete with the energy of life-force and cause trouble. If the life force's strength is strong, and its motion through the body is free and unabated, then life flows smoothly. You can face physical and psychological problems and stressful situations in life when it is weak, or if you are suffering from energy blockages.

3.2 How to perform Reiki?

Reiki for practitioners is primarily based on self-healing. You will want to learn more about doing Reiki while you are going on your Reiki path. This happens after Reiki level 2 where you'll be tuned to perform Reiki on others. It's important to remember that anytime you give Reiki to someone, you explain the nature of Reiki treatment accurately. In turn, this involves illustrating what you have learned in healing and practicing Reiki. Reiki treats triggers not signs. This will not happen overnight but can take many Reiki sessions to solve the root of the problem completely.

Furthermore, it is important to let the consumer thoroughly appreciate the 'cleaning time' beforehand. Symptoms growing get worse as the self-healing mechanisms of Reiki infiltrate the body and mind of the individual. Explain to the client that an individual in his or her life can experience adjustments, and that these may sometimes be significant. Through the method, they may find indications of their lives that would warn them what roads or actions they are meant to follow, what may not change their lives, and who prevents and eliminates their lives and restrains them from doing those events might make them happier. It's necessary to explain this in detail or a patient may get frightened and will stop getting Reiki therapy.

Check to figure out whether a person really needs healing. Many people just don't want to get, look healthier or get healed for any unexplained cause. A practitioner must engage in a lengthy discussion with the client to allow him to determine from Reiki what their primary objective is. When an individual does not wish to be cured, Reiki would have little effect on them.

3.3 Reiki's Success

Across other health-care settings, including clinics, Reiki has been introduced in recent years, too. UMN, that is, the University of Minnesota's Center for Spirituality & Healing, hands out similar evidence from some of Reiki's more clinically based research. It shows that this holistic treatment plays a vital role in decreasing anxiety and pain, promoting relaxation, increasing exhaustion and helping to relieve depression symptoms.

3.4 Underlying Principles of Reiki

Reiki Doctrine dates back to the late nineteenth or early twentieth century, and the teachings of Mikao Usui, a Japanese monk. Usui is basing his healing approaches on strategies and theories derived from many traditional Asian healing practices, according to the Langone Medical Center of New York University.

At the center of Reiki is the theory-once accepted in Western medicine in the Middle Ages and now prevalent in Eastern medicine today-that disease is caused by imbalances in the essential energies of the body and that correcting these imbalances promotes recovery, according to the Spirituality & Recovery Center of UMN.

This ancient idea of an inexhaustible reservoir of energy that can be harnessed for healing is believed to have "rediscovered" Usui. A Reiki practitioner (the first was Usui) could even instruct others to practice this calming force by a process named attunements.

Its use is not based on one's intellectual ability or spiritual growth, and is therefore available to all. Tens of thousands of people of all ages and backgrounds were taught effectively.

While Reiki is metaphysical fundamentally it is not a religion. It has no dogma, and there's no obligation to have a specific belief for any person to know about Reiki or use it. However, Reiki is not at all based on trust, and will function whether you believe in it or not. Because Reiki comes from God, many people feel that using Reiki puts them in more contact with their religious experience than having only an abstract understanding of it.

While Reiki is not a religion, it is still very practical in the Reiki approach to live and conduct in a way that encourages harmony with others. Mikao Usui, the inventor of Reiki's natural healing process, proposed that to promote peace and unity, which are almost common in all societies, one must obey certain simple ethical values.

3.5 Reiki in Action

During a Reiki therapy session a patient is usually lying on a massage table. According to Baldwin, the Reiki practitioner puts his or her hands in various locations over (or simply on top of) the patient's body, starting at the head crown. The Reiki energy flows through the practitioner from [his or her] hands to the person lying on the bed. However, the exact process by which the Reiki energy supposedly flows from one person to another is unknown. So certain Reiki practitioners claim they can treat people without getting anywhere near them — a method known as "distance healing." Some of the hypotheses of Reiki therapy is that Reiki should be linked to electromagnetic radiation so interact through a person's electromagnetic field. According to UMN's Spirituality & Healing Center, one theory is that Reiki causes relaxing, which in turn decreases a patient's exposure to pain and promotes healing.

Reiki stimulates energy (Reiki) inside the body for movement. You have strength in the body but it can be diverted and not moving quickly. During or after a procedure you may feel the effects of unblocked energy. Physical and psychological symptoms will intensify for a while, as the mind / body purify itself. So if anything happens to you, just ride it out and realize that the suffering will pass and you will quickly feel much stronger. This is important that you assist your body the best you can and help you get beyond the cleaning process.

Reiki does not steer or regulate the energies of life force in any way-it 's about removing the contaminants that hinder the free flow of energy. Interestingly, the skill to use Reiki is not "taught" but instead is transferred from instructor to student in a college. The patient is exposed to an "attunement," which helps the student to experience and move energy from life power. This is not a sacred activity so anybody who wants will learn Reiki without any religious convictions. The art of Reiki goes beyond medical injury care. The ideology urges one to live and act in ways that promote harmony both inside and with others. Getting the determination and commitment on self-improvement is an essential aspect of the Reiki teachings.

Both the teacher and the patient will assume responsibility for their own healing and the Reiki lessons are essential resources to lead a happy life. Here's a little glimpse of what Reiki is all about: said Mikao Usui:

I won't get upset just for today.

Just for today I'm not going to think.

On this very day I shall be grateful for all my blessings.

I can just operate for today with integrity and authenticity.

For today I would only be kind to all human things.

That is so perfect that you don't need to be ideal all the time-because you can do both of things on only one day.

3.6 Evidence on Reiki Effectiveness

Most medical therapies are tested through what is considered a placebo-controlled, double-blind trial. Patient groups are given either a real treatment or a false treatment (such as a sugar pill) in those studies. Neither the study participants nor the researchers themselves knew which patients received the real thing, and which received a so-called "sham treatment," according to Langone Medical Center.

However, a double-blind Reiki test cannot be performed, because the person delivering the treatment will eventually need to know if he or she is doing the real thing or a placebo treatment.

Research, for example, demonstrates Reiki's effectiveness in decreasing fear in women suffering from hysterectomies and minimizing discomfort among persons with chronic illness.

In fact, Reiki masters aren't claiming to heal everything their patients suffer from. Of starters, when Reiki is used on cancer victims, it's not about tumor healing. It's about helping the individual feel more relaxed, and growing their fear and discomfort. A recent analysis by researchers at the University of Pennsylvania finds that Reiki really plays the function for people recovering from cancer.

After decades of often disputed legitimacy, Reiki's efficacy as positive energy treatment is attracting fresh recognition within the scientific community. Not only are highly accredited medical facilities across the United States providing patients with holistic therapeutic services such as Reiki, these facilities evaluate the outcomes of their services and apply them for analysis and collection. The outcomes of these Reiki studies are nothing short of amazing.

3.7 Why Reiki Has Been Discounted

Reiki has been gazed at with disdain along with other therapeutic approaches to healing for years, including condemnation by scientific institutions, educators, traditional academics, and clergy. The idea that an invisible, etheric "life-force-energy" structure permeated or engulfed the human body was thought to be nothing short of nonsense. Such negative assumptions have been developed on the assumption that conventional science or scientific instruments "unseen" and "un-measurable" fields of "life force" such as those recognized as Chi or Qi in China, as Ki in Japan, and as Prana in India. All the animosity and competition, however, has shifted as a consequence of Reiki's proven efficacy.

The clinical, scientific, and research societies have rarely been granted a detailed set of directed, evidence-based practice. It wasn't until 2005 that William Lee Rand formed Center for Reiki Study. He created the Reiki Education International Center, and later became the chairman of this organization. He was also a world pioneer in Reiki education, and developed what is now called the Touchstone Process.

In fact, the Touchstone Framework is a peer evaluation method that reviews the latest status of clinical work on Reiki services in schools, facilities, and institutions throughout the United States. The process of measurement is rigorous, unbiased and accurate and it integrates the current empirical testing activities. William Lee Rand started to develop The Touchstone Project after developing the Reiki in Hospitals platform, which is known to be the most comprehensive list of hospitals offering Reiki services worldwide. At Touchstone the process is different. Just too many reputable Reiki reports have been historically compiled, checked, and analyzed through a common source.

3.8 Reiki case studies

The latest data analyzed (from 2008-2009) provide clear evidence that in humans and animals Reiki is indeed responsible for a positive biological response. The strongest proof (rated as "excellent" in the Process) in laboratory rats was reported in the most carefully monitored of all experiments. Reiki therapies were obtained on stressed-out laboratory rats in both 2006 and 2008, and both showed significantly reduced reactions to stress, anxiety and depression. The placebo party provided fake Reiki therapy, and no decrease in pain, anxiety or depression was recorded. Human studies conducted between 1993 and 2006 showed scores ranging from Satisfactory to Outstanding, both indicating that Reiki therapy results have been successful in managing rates of human pain. There were some hospital-typical "confounding factors" (as opposed to laboratory) studies; however, comparatively, the Reiki placebo therapies in this experiment were unsuccessful in pain management. For Reiki work you can find many examples of Reiki studies conducted in hospitals and universities.

3.9 Vital Signs

New York-Presbyterian Hospital / Columbia University Campus performed one of the first researches ever undertaken to determine the efficacy of Reiki therapy on the autonomic nervous system. This "free, spontaneous analysis" involved a group of Reiki therapies, a group of "sham" therapies and a group of "controls." The test started with all subjects at the stage of the "baseline" autonomic nervous system. The findings of the Reiki group therapy showed a decrease in heart rate, respiration and blood pressure. These promising findings provoked the team to suggest additional, broader research to explore the biological effects of Reiki treatment. It is important to note that Columbia was one of the first hospitals in their Integrative Medicine Program (CIMP) that offered Reiki.

3.10 The Reiki Experience

Reiki is a marvelous therapeutic power, and the most positive approach to transform lives. When you choose to receive therapies or become a Reiki practitioner, your life can become more peaceful and simple. Can you feel this vibration while you're doing a Reiki session? Many people do, and some do not. If you are connected to your body, and the energy that passes into it, you will feel a pleasant glow or radiance. And you can't sense much at all and only feel at peace at ease. Reiki is a balanced, strength- or metaphysical way of healing. Nearly all ailments and disorders may be healed or strengthened using Reiki, and it is a great alternative to Western conventional treatments as it has minimal adverse effects and promotes a positive, confident mindset that is important for recovery. Mindset is crucially necessary. The contaminants that interfere with life-force energy are emotions such as anger, jealousy, feelings of humiliation, sadness, shame, fear or frustration. The body cannot be viewed as composed only of material objects – it's a combination between the human body and the thoughts / spirits. It all makes up "you." Reiki operates holistically to make the true you come through — without the mental and physical toxins. Reiki is a soft and powerful therapeutic tool that activates the body's inherent capacity to cure itself. As a natural healing mechanism, it can help everyone, from young babies to adults and it is a healthy, non-invasive procedure. A drug represents a stunning, dazzling radiance that shines through and around you. Reiki activates the whole individual, including body, thoughts, mind and spirit, creating numerous beneficial results including sensations of tranquility and comfort along with protection and well-being. Others reported miraculous discoveries. Reiki is a basic, natural, and healthy therapeutic practice of healing and self-improvement which anyone can use. This has been effective in curing almost any documented disease and sickness, and is still useful. That, in conjunction with all other treatment or recovery methods, also tends to relieve adverse effects and promote cure. In a safe and compassionate environment, Reiki treatments provide you with the ability to relax and re - balance fully.

Reiki often lets the body attain an inner balance at all stages, both physically, psychologically and spiritually. Along with the recovery of other physical conditions, it will also promote the reversal of some destructive behavioral patterns, turning them into more positive and productive thought styles. Reiki energy is delicate to receive but a powerful process of relaxation should be used at all times and the results can be experienced immediately. Reiki has grown in popularity over the past few years, and is being practiced by several holistic practitioners. This has been widely accepted by conventional doctors and consultants, leading to some hospitals that require Reiki practitioners to work with doctors to assist their patients.

3.11 Reiki Therapy and Benefits

Reiki therapies are suitable for all as a natural healing device, from young babies to adults, since this is a healthy, non-invasive procedure. These can be combined alongside other conventional or complementary therapies. Reiki can be done on a recovery sofa, or sitting in a chair, and seeking treatment is convenient. Treatments are ideal for people who are simply involved in de-stress, or those who might have an injury or an incident. Reiki should be used as a calming therapy that allows the body, mind and emotions to relax. There are no established contraindications of Reiki having been healed. A certified practitioner, though, may always take a short medical history from you before recovery starts and will review it with you at the outset if any concerns occur.

If you have any medical issues, please call your doctor during the initial consultation. Reiki supplements conventional medical practice as well as other alternative therapies, though the disorder may be serious. There are no promises to be willing to cure you fully by Reiki, but there are several instances when that has occurred. Whatever you may want care for, Reiki can certainly help in some way on so many levels. It may also be time to look for methods to help you live in this better state once you have made changes, such as altering old negative patterns of understanding, enhancing ways to cope with stress, improving your health, getting more exercise and so on.

Reiki Promotes Harmony and Balance

It assists in cultivating peace, harmony and order. This is an important, non-invasive source of healing energy that strengthens the body's natural healing capacity while simultaneously energizing and promoting the overall wellness of body. Reiki primarily works at maintaining balance at all stages and explicitly focuses on the illness and condition rather than simply masking or alleviating symptoms.

He implies a balance of intellectual and emotional, brain left & right side, feminine and masculine, labeling it as good/evil, optimistic/pessimistic, etc. while the therapist talks with the customer.

Reduces Stress and Anxiety

What a lot of people enjoy in a Reiki session is that it let them make room for themselves while they're not performing 'just' being.' After Reiki treatment, clients recorded feeling happier, more relaxed, peaceful, and lighter.

Space is offered by Reiki where you can become aware of what's going on the inner of your mind and body. You learn to start listening to your body from this place and make smart decisions about your health.

More presentness means that you are inside your body and which allows you to gain even greater insight into the inner consciousness and intellect that is present in all.

Fosters Equilibrium between Spirit, Mind & Body

Reiki Regular sessions will offer a more calm and comfortable state. In this state, a person can cope with daily stress better. The mental balance like this also increases thought, memory, and clear-mindedness.

Reiki can treat wounds of emotional/mental and also helps in ease mood, anxiety, irritation, and even rage changes. Reiki also will strengthen and restore intimate relationships.

Since Reiki increases your love capacity, it will open you to the around people and help you improve your ties.

Aids in Removing Body Toxins

A lot of time was spent by us in the stress-reactive process of fight/flight that our 'norm' it becomes and the bodies forget how the returning of balance.

Our bodies are reminded by Reiki of how to switch to the PNS (parasympathetic system) (rest/digest) mode of self-healing.

Rest/eat isn't just not getting active and getting good or achieving little.' It makes you sleep more and eat more, which is crucial to preserving safety and vitality. In this state, if more you're, the more engaged and productive you will be without getting overwhelmed or tired.

Reiki Enhances Concentration

Reiki helps you remain centered at the present, rather than caught up by previous errors or future anxieties. It will reinforce your willingness to embrace and deal with the ways things go, even if they do not meet your wishes or timetable. Instead of acting out of habit, you start to respond positively to circumstances, to people, and yourself.

Helps in Sleeping Better

The best benefit of holding a session of Reiki is treating sleep disorders. Once we are relaxed, better we sleep, quick healing of our body, more clearly thinking by us, and we are more closely linked. During their session of Reiki, people will also feel immense relaxation or sometimes during the session of deep sleep.

Improves the self-healing power of the body

Reiki therapy quickly gets you back to your normal state or makes the body push in the correct direction at least.

This means your breath, blood pressure, and heart rate improved. Better and deeper breathing is the first thing that during self-practice can happen when someone else gets treatment. If we breathe better then naturally our minds relax. Science is backing the fact.

As your breathing deepens, your body changes into the PNS supremacy, that is the process of rest/digest. Instead of the fight/flight process that was observed more frequently. The body was developed to function mainly in the process of rest/digest.

Reiki is Pain-relieving

A Reiki therapy may look like merely a series of hand positions on the outside with a view to gazing in; it helps return balance to the lowest possible point. It helps your system improve your body's essential functions (sleeping, breathing, and digesting), so that you're physical processes work in the best possible way.

Reiki helps to alleviate migraine pain, sciatica, arthritis, etc. This also helps in signs of diabetes, severe fatigue, effects of menopause, and sleeplessness.

Reiki facilitates spiritual Development

To enjoy the rewards of Reiki, you don't need to engage in meditation. But others seek Reiki services to support people on their path of self-healing i.e., personal development/ spiritual growth.

Instead of focusing on individual symptoms, Reiki treats the person as a whole. It can bring about intense, sometimes subtle changes from within you. So how is it? Guidance for what to be done under difficult situations will arrive faster. Or it might cause a shift in belief or attitude about the situation of you. You see the situation suddenly from a new perspective and can handle it with greater confidence. Or it could lead to the right sort of action that's required and directed from within.

Reiki helps Medical Treatment

This is a perfect substitute to conventional medication which helps to emotionally and physically relax patients. If an individual feels assured the recovery cycle feels enhanced. After the Reiki sessions, it helps in better sleeping, and feel calmer.

The Reiki best thing is that non-invasive it is, and very gently delivered. The practitioner of Reiki can provide Reiki to people who have major injuries like burns or others without touching the body.

Reiki is also safe if medical conditions you have like diabetes, autism, diseases of the heart. You can get Reiki therapies if under chemotherapy you are. Pregnant women may get Reiki therapies to help them get easily past all phases of pregnancy. Reikis to everything!

Doing Reiki by yourself

Some can practice Reiki on their own. Some to Reiki, are drawn for supporting their physical rehabilitation and some are more eager to explore the personal development of the

Chapter 4: Reiki Attunement and Effects

Unlike the rest of the healing arts, Reiki is translated from mentor to student through a procedure known as Reiki attunement. This process of attunement allows the student to make a connection with the source of universal Reiki. In this cycle of attunement you are the source of Reiki. You get to be able to move Reiki energy both for yourself and others. While in an magzine or book you can read about Reiki and learn hand positions, you can't practice Reiki until you are tuned to Reiki channel.

4.1 Ceremony for Reiki Attunement

The process of Reiki attunement is the method by which one becomes a true practitioner of Reiki. Reiki tuning equips an individual with the power to access the energies of the Reiki (Universal Life Force) with ease. Once that ability has been acquired, it can then be used to heal a person or situation. It is important to note that only a Reiki master can give the attunements. For the purpose of training a person in Reiki, further tunings may be given. These attunements can also be given to someone for a larger Reiki experience as compared to other treatments usually experienced.

The method of the tuning is a ceremony for the spirit. In this ritual the Reiki master uses the Reiki symbols and other moves prescribed. This ritual generates a pattern of energy around the attunement receiver that reaches or attunes its energy field to the energies represented by the symbols. The attunement is irreversible, making the receiver a Reiki practitioner, even if the master uses the sign "subconscious." If this symbol is not being used then the entry is only temporary. In this rite the master starts by calming and centering himself. He instructs the receiver(s) to relax and level themselves. He says this ritual is about them, so that they will be willing and open to anything that comes their way. May it bring on any mood setting music, lights etc. The Master begins to stand before the recipients and he / she usually raises his / her hands high at shoulder height with palms facing forward. The receivers should be seated in a row with room around them, so that the Master can maneuver around them comfortably. The goal is to establish a safe passage to the sacred rite that follows. The Ceremony is made up of two sections. In the first part, the Reiki Master behind the receiver draws the Reiki symbols, and in the second half, the symbols are then drawn in front of the receiver.

4.2 Experiencing the Reiki Attunement

Receiving a Reiki treatment is a deep spiritual practice, since the internal channels are unlocked by a Reiki master. The strong opening enables the Reiki energies to move naturally through the body and reflect on the safety and the wellness of others.

The sensation created during a Reiki tuning is intimate, however as the pathways of Reiki energy are opened up, students often describe experiencing their body lightening and tingling from head to toe.

In brief, opening an attunement has the benefit of enhancing those outlets of healing and channeling energies, and students believe obtaining an attunement produces an increased emotional awareness and enhances some innate spiritual responsiveness.

4.3 Reiki Attunement's preparation

It depends on how you train for a Reiki tuning from your own unique spiritual practice. Opening an energetic track is not a matter of lightness, and while doing anything to prepare for a Reiki tuning is not purely important. Before being attuned, most students prefer to reconnect with their own spiritual practice, enhance the cumulative impact of the attunement and optimize their transformative strength. One recommended method for preparing for a Reiki tuning includes a 3-day cleanse before the tuning. Refrain from the consumption of heavy foods, restrict or remove caffeine, sugar, cigarettes or alcohol from your daily life. Spend your time reading or meditating, rather than watching TV. Consciously aim to cause these harmful feelings as anger or envy.

All of these exercises will enable you to embrace the spiritual change more effectively and enable the attunement to have significant long-term impacts on your life and wellbeing. Once you are tuned to Reiki the strength of Reiki can float into you for the rest of your life. Your power to harness and transfer Reiki energy is with you, as the gift of Reiki guides you and supports you throughout your entire life.

4.4   Advantages   of   Remotely   Received Attunements

In-person courses are sometimes conducted rapidly, with the students getting no opportunity to learn the content. The attunements are given in masse at the close of the term. That provides very little time for the students to plan for the fundamental spiritual transition suggested by an attunement. By studying online, you'll be able to grasp and incorporate the effects of Reiki at your own speed and take a few days to plan for the tuning before you receive it.

Reiki is an intensive practice, so for the remainder of your life, much of the Reiki you seek so give should be at a place. Making the Reiki trip from a distance makes you prepare a boundless Reiki-life.

4.5 Experience after Attunement

Reiki tuning is a power-up procedure in which a master passes the Reiki energy to their pupil. The procedure unblocks multiple points in the body which are called "chakras," enabling the energies of the fundamental life force to pass across the whole body. After this attunement cycle the student will monitor the positive force of Reiki.

These tunings cause regeneration and purification of the receiver's body during the next four stages, culminating of improvements that the recipient experiences during the same stages.

Detoxifies Physically

Following a tuning the washing procedure begins in the body to eliminate toxins. This healing period continues for 21 days, comprising of 3 to 7 chakra periods in which the force of Reiki travels across the seven chakras and enhances the release of energy by through these energy points. The body can experience certain physical adjustments through this detoxification, such as mood fluctuations, fatigue, diarrhea, vomiting, stomach pain, etc., these are considered Reiki detoxification effects, which are cured as the procedure begin.

Heals Spiritually

An attunement has a profound impact spiritually during which a patient is allowed to undergo changes in attitudes of friends and family. As for relationships, moral and social beliefs, an individual may also experience a change in his views. During any point you can feel anxious or frustrated, but remember, that is completely ordinary and you have to calm down. You just have to continue practicing Reiki and this will help you find out that while everything seems to have altered but much simpler and more understandable as your way of life has been revolutionized by the energy of the spiritually driven life force, and you have accomplished tremendous spiritual development.

Cleanses Emotionally

During the cleansing; on an emotional perspective, a person may feel powerful emotions such as feelings of depression, anger, isolation and so forth. These emotions have been kept deep within yourself from previous experiences. There might be no obvious cause for such emotions to emerge that may mislead many people, but looking at reality, it is the common life-force energies that remove you from these deeply seeded heavy pressures to fill you with positivity and guide your emotions into the road of recovery.

In order to support yourself during this process, you can perform Reiki while you imagine that all these negative emotions are pouring out of you via solar plexus. You may also prepare a hot bath for yourself to aid in emotional relaxation.

Purifies Mentally

As mental detoxification begins, as they come back to you, you can feel your current lifestyle disrupted by long-lost behaviors and behavioral forms, including the desire for caffeine, alcohol and assorted foods, and so forth. Negative feelings will emerge like self-destruction, guilt, disappointment, etc. but don't be distracted, so it's finally time to let those fuzzy feelings and impulses quit you forever. You just need to spend time in a peaceful spot alone, practicing various meditations that will help guide your way of life and way of life towards an optimistic destination.

The insight will aid in realizing what improvements are to be made in your daily environment, what ideas and habits you need to know to achieve a better state of health. After receiving all attunements, your body's channels of energy will remain extended with the flow of positive life force energy for the remaining duration of your life.

The Reiki Pulse

You can feel the pulsating feeling of Reiki in all areas of your body, particularly in your hands' palms. Palms are the sources of Reiki power. Reiki is similar to a worried parent waiting for her beloved child to return, with open arms at the door. Reiki helps you bring your hands to good work. Reiki immediately turns on as long as you put your hands on your own body or anyone else's.

When you are adjusted with Reiki, you turn into living magnet of sorts. When you're close to someone who's

Reiki-receptive, your body can start heating up and spew out calming energies. This sensation will overpower the freshly tuned individual, particularly because this might happen because they were not previously recommended to. It could be your initial answer to put your palms on the victim but this isn't suggested. Always accept that you have absolutely no right to walk to a human and manipulate them simply because your body experiences convince you that they are responsive to it. You will still get approval before you do something like this.

Reiki Awareness

You don't need to touch anyone to start Reiki flowing over to them. A little smile will be enough as Reiki will then start the transferring. You also need to be mindful of the reality that you're a medium for Reiki. The receiving person need not be conscious that something is going on. If you're in a group of people, like sitting in a movie theater or market shopping, you're probably not going to be sure who the Reiki really flows into. Accept your Reiki position as a conduit, and don't get tangled in a mentality of needing to know who is receiving, this will disturb your mentality. Just let it pour in. You won't really pay notice after some time when Reiki spreads through you, as it would become a natural activity. Healers acquainted with the healing prowess of stones may also integrate the relaxing forces of different crystals through their Reiki practice. In the other side, metals let energy flow and can consume Reiki, theoretically leveraging the maximum benefit for the receiver. Magnetic jewelry is also a nuisance, as the Reiki force may be distorted.

Reiki Energy in your palms

There might be instances when Reiki can ball in the palms, producing an energy aura that circles around. It is like having a regular tennis ball attached to your palm. You can't shake it off even by vigorous movement. Look at this ball as a living thing with a heartbeat.

Having to experience these tennis ball like pulsating organisms might be a strange or even alarming experience, but there is no cause for concern. Reiki doesn't flow outside of you as it can't go anywhere. But this shows that Self-Reiki is required. Using this strong abundance in your mouth, and put your hands on yourself. Enabling Reiki to circulate through your body will help minimize or let loose the energy from your hand.

Reiki can be applied to Objects

You will take full advantage of this by infusing Reiki with inanimate objects, as you sense a large amount of energy build inside your body. Reiki can turn objects into healing tools by transferring Reiki into them. Reiki can be placed in anything by placing the object between your palms and letting Reiki energy to transfer into it. Reiki Stage II practitioners can even put Reiki symbols alongside their energy in these objects, making the objects even more potent.

Reiki can fill any of the following objects:

• Your sleeping pillow; your sleep will be very relaxing.

• Your bathing water; your bath will be more soothing.

• Your light bulbs and lamps; their lighting will have a Reiki glow!

• Scented candles, floral essences, and incense sticks.

• The shampoo, toothpaste, and skin lotions.

• Reiki your recommended medicine and vitamins.

• Your shoes; they will become very comforting.

• Reiki your machine to help avoid every device crash.

• Reiki your phone and be more patient with noisy phone calls.

Vibration in Hands

Pipes stretch and contract, adapting to the water that flows into them. Your body always responds in the same way to the Reiki flow which is channeled into your body. You can feel your hands vibrating as Reiki flows out from your hands at a greater pace or more than you're used to. The sensation results from the Reiki flowing into your body so fast it gets back into your palms. Reiki is attempting to smash out and head where it wants to head to, but the gaps in your hands are too tiny to allow Reiki to pass on effectively.

That isn't an insurmountable issue. You haven't done anything wrong so there isn't any reason to worry too hard about it. Besides being awkward, your vibrating hands merely mean that the receiver is in great need of it. Reiki's receivers sponges as soon as they can obtain it.

Post-Reiki Sensations

You can even sense pain in your wrists and finger joints along with the sensation of vibration in your neck. Around your neck, shoulders and even down your sides, you will feel a heavy pull of Reiki energy when helping patients with severe illnesses. If channeling large amounts of Reiki when healing others becomes challenging or uncomfortable, withdraw hands from the receiver regularly and allow your hands some time to relax. For 10 minutes, you can switch hands on, for 10 minutes you can turn the hands off etc.

Feeling of Flow of Reiki Energy like a river

Typically Reiki flows toward the easiest route. When the normal flow of a flowing river encounters a water dam, the stream gathers up in that place before either it smashes past the obstruction or it re-routes itself by heading through it, flowing into the nearest clear path.

Reiki is analogous to a river. Its energy flows through us, filling us in the most likely way. Palm placements which are used to channel Reiki permits the energy to reach the body via various channels.

Twelve can hand placements are used to provide a complete body Reiki procedure. The four placements are on the head, four of them are on the front side of the body and four hand placings are on the back. Reiki for 5 minutes at every one of these placements aids in spreading Reiki uniformly around the whole body. When the palms are positioned at one location, the person also encounters hot spots somewhere else. You might touching the person's chest, and the person might feel a trickle of energy flowing down their legs. You have to know Reiki always follows its path and its destination.

Deals with blockages and bottlenecks

You can reach a location on the body that seems clogged even by moving your palms through various hand placements. If you don't feel that Reiki is poring out from your hands, your first reaction could be to try a different placement-but hang on. Obstructed places are denser, so they need to focus more, too. All you should do more often is move your hands a few inches from the spot, for Reiki to flow once again. If it's not working so be careful. Hold your palms on the body of the receiver, where you know that the Reiki is obstructed five minutes before you pass on.

Creates Harmony with your Hand

In delivering Reiki to a body, no burden should be placed. Put your palms, softly, on the neck. There may be circumstances where your hands may feel as though when you give Reiki, they actually sink deep inside the body. This feeling of pulling or sinking takes place as the etheric hand reaches into the body's deep tissues.

In a Reiki session, you will catch a waft of scent. It is suggested that this could be a sign that an Ascended Master, an angel, or a spirit is leading the session. There has been mention of feeling Takata sensei's presence by a delicate floral scent.

Withdrawing your physical hand to join can trigger a healing session interruption until your etheric hand has withdrawn itself. This form of deeper healing is likely to occur if your hands feel like they're attached to the body. It's helpful when doing this deeper healing work, keeping your palms in place for an extended time. When owing to time limitations or some such unfortunate reason you can't keep your hands in place, make sure to slowly withdraw your hands without some drastic measures. Make sure that they are as friendly as possible.

Reiki has unlimited energy

You give your effort and time to help when you give someone a Reiki treatment: You don't send away your own strength. Reiki supply is unlimited. It will not stop any time. A Reiki professional, you present yourself as a platform to get Reiki from.

You can have many feeling during or even after a session of Reiki. These feelings can range from tiredness to excitement. However, those sentiments did not arise because you were deprived of strength. Something more is happening. You may have been deprived of Reiki yourself, and you have also got Reiki by offering Reiki to someone else. Reiki should always listen to the practitioner along with the client's needs. Reiki can become a treatment for both. If you often feel drained after offering Reiki to a patient, this is a sign that you need to spend some time on treating yourself.

You become Empathetic

If an individual is empathetic about the sufferings and difficulties of others, it may contribute to the creation of mirrored illnesses. Possessing empathic ability, though, is not necessarily needed for Reiki and neither does it improve Reiki's effectiveness. People with empathy ought to realize that the desire to "carry in" or "sense" someone else's suffering or emotions is not being utilized as a device to diagnose. Do not hang on to these feelings –you should let them go as soon as possible. When you feel the effects of someone else's pains or emotions inside yourself, take a few calm, deep breaths; then ask the patient to also do the same. This will aid in breaking down the energy that has been trapped so that treatment can proceed without further pain.

Chapter 5: Reiki Symbols

Reiki's symbols are like keys which unlock the doors to a higher consciousness. You can also see them as buttons, and when you press the button, you get an immediate response. One of the functions of the Reiki symbol is to bypass the user's precognition that such things cannot be achieved (i.e., distance healing) immediately. The symbols activate a belief or purpose built into the symbols, which helps the user obtain the results expected. The various symbols also easily connect the individual to the common life-force.

When a Reiki Master makes an attunement and shows the Reiki symbols to a student, the shape of the symbol is ingrained in the students' mind and fuses with the spiritual forces it represents. When a Reiki practitioner makes images, finds a sign, or visualizes it, it can automatically communicate with the forces it reflects. During the numerous Reiki Attunements three Reiki symbols are given in "traditional" Reiki. They are:

- The Power Symbol (Choku Rei)
- The Mental/Emotional symbol (Sei He Ki)

- The symbol of distance (Hon Sha Zi Sho Nen)

5.1 The Three Reiki Symbols

The Reiki symbols are partially based on Kanji, the Japanese form of writing. The images can be created or visualized, as demonstrated during the Reiki Attunements. That would mean that there will be a number of variations between the signals given by various Masters as more and more citizens are tuned to Reiki. It is not necessarily a concern because there is no 100 percent right or wrong way to design them. However, the Reiki symbols offered to a student should act as they combine the intent and the relation with the spiritual forces that it represents.

The Reiki Power symbol – Choku Rei

Choku Rei is spoken as "Cho-Koo-Ray."
Choku Rei 's basic translation is: "Put the force of the cosmos in here."

The Power symbol can be used in increasing the power of Reiki. It can also be used for protection. See it as a light switch helping to boost the capacity to immediately harness Reiki energy.

Draw or imagine the symbol before you and you will have immediate access to the additional healing energies. When used together, Choku Rei often gives more power to the other symbols.

The symbol can be used at any time during a process but it is particularly useful when used at the beginning of a session to activate the Reiki energy.

If you choose to attach different "functions" to the Power symbol then only make a clear comment and intent on what you intend to do with the symbol, and it will do it for you.

Uses of Choku Rei

• Make your healing skills better; use it as a light switch.

• The Reiki energies should be concentrated on one particular point of the body. (Draw or imagine Choku Rei in front of you, or draw it in your hands if you like.) Draw the symbol directly from the location you specify.

- Increase the influence of certain symbols by drawing the symbols before drawing them elsewhere.

- The Power symbol can be used in closing the gap around the receiver to prevent the energy gained from escaping the body. Draw it over the body with the intent of sealing the healing process.

- The Sign of Strength can be used in cleansing spiritually a space from harmful energies, to make it light and sacred place. Draw the symbols to energize space on all the walls, ceilings , and floors.

- Harmful energy can be removed from crystals and other objects; to clean it, draw the power symbol on the crystal or object, and return it to its original state. Keep the item in your hands, then send it to Reiki.

- Shield yourself from negative energies such as those you treat, or anybody you meet. Draw or visualize the Reiki Power symbol before you, in order to be absolutely free.

- Protect yourself, family, partner, house and everything you love. Simply draw Choku Rei directly onto the object / person you want to protect him / her from harm. Since Reiki operates on all different levels of existence, it will provide security at all levels of existence as well, of course. There are only a few implementations. For the Reiki Power – Choku Rei symbol you can use your own intuition and imagination to look for various applications. There are no limits on what you may do. Just note, all of the power is in your head, let the symbols' function guide your simple intent. Students in Reiki 1 should continue to use the symbol Power. Choku Rei is usually drawn in an anti-clockwise (from left to right) direction. Others prefer to draw it in the form of the clockwise, since it seems to suit them better, and it often seems more logical. There's no way that's right or wrong; deciding on the position is your decision, so please do what's best for you. The horizontal line stands for Reiki's origins.

Sei He Ki

Currently, Sei He Ki's is usually pronounced like "Say-Hay-Key."

Sei He Ki's literal meaning is: "Man and God become one. "Typically, the symbol of Mental/Emotional

 together brings the "brain and body." It facilitates and helps people not only bring

mental and emotional issues to surface but also helps to reduce the emotional and mental causes of their major problems. Many citizens have come to understand together with physicians that much of our illnesses are focused on our behavioral and emotional imbalances. This problem is compounded by our ignorance of the stated question. The symbol works as a powerful force, and focuses on the issue. Subsequently the subconscious harmonizes with the physical side. Sei He Ki can also be used for mental and emotional healing aids. Sei He Ki balances the brain's left and right, and gives peace and harmony. Sei He Ki is also very helpful when it comes to relationship issues. It can also be used to fix various issues including fear, depression, nervousness, sadness, and anger.

Uses of Sei He Ki

Sei He Ki can be used to help heal drug abuse, smoking, and alcohol.
• Can be used for weight reduction.
• You can use Sei He Ki to locate things you've misplaced. Only sketch the sign before you and ask for guidance in identifying the stuff incorrect.

• You will use this icon to boost your recall when reading and learning. Just draw the icon on each page while you read it, in order to recall the relevant sections.

• When you do healing (normal or distance), you should always add the sign, because that will aid the healing process. There are many mental / emotional roots to many physical problems.

Sei He Ki is directly linked to Yin and Yang, and the two sides of the brain equilibrium.

A part of the sign is reserved to Yang. Our left brain hand is related to logical thought, order, and reasoning. Yin is considered the symbol's right hand, because it's aligned with perception, emotions, because creativity. When you approach someone else and visualize the symbol's left hand, i.e. the Yang part of the sign, so the receiver's brain winds up on the recipient's right side.

Hon Sha Zi Sho Nen

It is pronounced usually as "Hon-Shaa-Zie-Show-Nen". A meaning generally of the symbol is: "No past, present, or future" it may have the sense "the Buddha inside me contacts inside Buddha of you."

The symbol of Distance, as suggested by its name, may be used to transmit energy over some distance. Distance and time do not present any issue when this sign for Reiki is used. Several practitioners consider the symbol Hon Sha Zi Sho Nen of maximum use and strength.

The symbol provide offers links to "Akashic Archives," the life history of each person. So it can be used to cure karmic. By using this symbol, trauma, and different life experiences, past lives, or parallel ones can be highlighted and released which influence and mirror the behaviors of peoples.

If you do distance healing, you should be responsive! Don't concentrate your energies to solve a common headache issue. Return infinite resources of Reiki when they go where wanted most they are. When performing distance healing, energies are going to work on user's subtle body, the Aura, and the Chakras and not on a physical level that much, i.e., seeing the body & relieving pain, for example, sometime might be taken for the energies.

The person to whom you are going to send Reiki will feel likely happening it. In fact, if a person has an active mind, he or she would be able to tell you what you did and why you did it.

The hands-on therapy is not needed nearly by distance healing. You just need some mins to send away healing. If you wish, you may set up distance healing of Reiki to automatically replicate the energy transmitted to a human. You are putting on the repeat, a limit of time because else it might run indefinitely. You should also schedule it each alternative day for renewing and empowering distance healing. Just remember that it's your intention to guide what happens!

Uses of Hon Sha Zi Sho Nen

Some of the uses of Sha Ze Sho Nen are:

Sha Zi Sho Nen Heals the Past

If in some past you submit Reiki messages to help you cope with "dead wounds" that could bother you in current, so it can help you obtain the desired effects. Although it won't reverse the circumstances, because past experiences cannot be reversed, submitting past Reiki because part of the healing process tends to reshape the whole encounter. It also helps in pain healing and helps you move forward with a life of yours.

Sha Zi Sho Nen improves conditions of future

Using the potential distance calming sign helps preserve the energy of Reiki like some battery that will be activated at a moment you need it. Reiki sending for medical visits, interviews, tests, seminars or travel in advance will help to adapt to the unpredictable future situations and maintain an optimistic and open attitude.

Sha Zi Sho Nen Heals Across The Space and Time

The distance healing Reiki symbol is primarily used in sending healing energy through a place, area, to different country parts, or even it can be sent in the world anywhere. All of this will have the intention of helping those who are not around you. It is often otherwise called the symbol of "absent healing".

Most Reiki practitioners find the Reiki interval healing sign very powerful and efficient signals. However, when this symbol is used it is worth noting that energies in lengthy distance healing used will more effectively work on the individual subtle body such as the chakras or the aura, instead of acting directly on a physical body of a person.

Energies used mostly for remote healing take time for working on the body (physical) and help ease physical pain or strain; sending the energy of Reiki for a specific problem like backaches or headaches will significantly control the energies. The strongest approach is to provide Reiki to a patient and that would encourage the flow of energy directly through the body area that it is most desired.

Periodically encouraging the daily healing of long-distance plays an important role in making the energies positively work successfully. It is also worth remembering that Reiki can't be used in changing a person or behavior of him/her. The Reiki wisdom knows what for the person is best, and energies function accordingly to the good possible result.

How to accomplish Reiki Distance Healing

There are several ways of sending Reiki, and different Reiki Masters may be using different methods. Most practitioners study a technique, which is then changed to suit their style, and then personalized. The below steps describe a technique that is considered successful by many people.

Step no. 1

The symbol of power is activated.

Step no. 2

The name or state of the receiver is written to whom you are transferring energy on a sheet of paper. Then hold your hands in between the paper.

Step no. 3

Hon Sha Zi Sho Nen symbol is drawn above the paper, in the air and 3 times repeat it.

Step no. 4

Recipient's name or circumstance are repeated. Draw the symbol of power.

Step no. 5

Let Reiki for the highest and greatest good, to flow to the recipient.

Step no. 6

The session of Reiki is finished by either hand clapping or actively shaking them to sever the touch.

A distant healing alternative approach is to use their image or a proxy (any object or a soft toy) despite writing on a paper piece with the name of them.

Dai Ko Myo-Sacred Master Reiki symbol

The Dai Ko Myo is considered in Usui Reiki to be the emblem of "lord." It is the significant most things in Reiki and can be seen only by Masters of Reiki. The influence of the symbol of Reiki Master takes on the impact of symbols, the first 3.

The most vibrating icon is Dai Ko Myo. Therefore, the most spiritually transformative. Use this image tends to facilitate the regeneration as energies, of the soul, are transferred to the further fragile aura layers and the chakras beyond. When the Holy Spirit is restored, there is always complete regeneration of the spiritual and the physical.

The Dai Ko Myo symbol helps also to restore our karma. Also recognized as the emblem of "the all-purpose sign of regeneration" and "the icon of liberation," this image of Reiki reflects everything about Reiki, that is, spiritual strength and devotion. At all levels, Reiki practitioners are given the master symbol by their Reiki teacher during tuning.

Dai Ko Myo Defined

The strength it symbolizes, which it holds when translating the individual symbols of the Reiki material symbol. While the meaning of "Dai" is big and great. "Ko" means seamless or shiny, "Myo" meaning is a bright light. Also, the symbol has been translated as obvious or simple and is for understanding and learning. The basic meaning of Dai Ko Myo is "Bright Light Shining" or "Great Enlightenment". This symbol of Reiki stands for inner wisdom, truth, and illumination.

Attunement of Dai Ko Myo

When a Reiki practitioner is adjusted to this symbol by a Reiki practitioner, the image hits the crown chakra and illuminates the essence of who we actually are. The icon commemorates both our divinity and membership, giving us closer to Heaven.

The Dai Ko Myo picture takes us back to the inherent divinity inside us, which helps us to cure ourselves and others. After initialization of the symbol it is highly advised that you include the symbol with all of your Reiki functions. It will motivate your ability to get an extra boost and allow you pull strong strength from your energetic network continuously.

Dai Ko Myo Activation

The symbol can be triggered in many ways, including but not limited to:

- Drawing it with your palm center
- By visualizing it
- Drawing the symbol with your finger
- Drawing it with your third eye
- Defining the symbol name three times
- Adding the Dai Ko Myo symbol to Reiki Healing

The use of the Reiki master symbol improves each form's healing effects. The symbol is normally used by Reiki for any healing, be it an individual or a group, hands-on or remote, or when aimed at an entity, item, or circumstance. Just draw the symbol of Reiki on your own hands or palms, and then assume. You can also redraw the symbol on the chakra of the crown and the palms or hands of the client, and the healing region.

Uses of Dai Ko Myo

- Used by Reiki masters for opening paths during Reiki settings and settling others who wish to become Reiki practitioners
- Helps strengthen the relationship between the practitioner and the divine forces.
- Heals the chakras, the aura and any disease that starts with our subconscious beliefs
- Helping our divine self-heal illness and disease.
- Improves immune function and boosts energy transfer through the body
- May be used to boost the curative efficacy of tinctures, medications or homeopathic remedies
- It helps to enlighten and to become more intuitive and psychic
- Can be used in all Reiki healings to create a refined and higher light dimension
- It may also be used to pull away physical, social, behavioral or metaphysical toxic energies from the body. This instead replaces the other ones.
- This helps build and strengthen self-consciousness, spiritual wellbeing and insight and personal growth.
- Using the symbol with other Reiki symbols helps improve performance. For example, using Dai Ko Myo with the remote healing symbol helps to move

energy quickly from the heart chakra of the healer to the heart chakra of the recipient.

- It may be used for crystal clearing or crystal charging. It can also be used to create self-healing crystals.
- It helps to improve immune function and, precisely for this reason, it is designed as an immune energizer. It also enhances the energy transfer into the body
- It may be used to improve the healing properties of herbal tinctures, medicinal products or homeopathic remedies.

Benefits of Dai Ko Myo symbol

Through changing yourself and guiding your life specifically to this goal, Dai Ko Myo makes you support others. Meditating on the symbol not only offers a spiritual measure of self-purification and self-cleansing, it also helps to create more peace and balance in your daily life. It adds "light" to your life, and helps remove physical, social, mental, and spiritual, current, past, and future blockages at all levels.

Dai Ko Myo is among the Reiki's most sacred depictions. The primary purpose of using this symbol is strength, enlightenment, peace and the awakening of the soul. It's a warm, luminous light that fills and nourishes, demonstrates the way and rests the soul. It helps protect the body & mind and it therefore encourages us to do the same. Using Dai Ko Myo can literally make significant benefits to life and make you a happier person.

CHAPTER 6: Reiki and Role of Seven Chakras

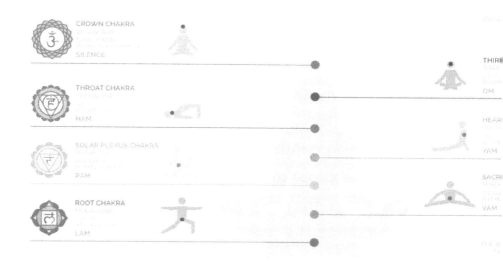

THE CHAKRAS
ENERGY HEALING

Although most people have heard of seven chakras, in fact there are 114 in the body. The human body is a complicated type of energy; besides the 114 chakras it also has 72,000 "Nadis," or energy channels, through which important energy, or "prana," passes. When the Nadis intersect at different points inside the body they form a triangle. We call this triangle a chakra which means "wheel." We call it a wheel because it symbolizes creation, dynamism, and movement. So we call it a chakra, although it is merely a triangle. Some of those centers are very powerful, whereas others are less strong. Those energy channels generate various properties on different levels inside a human being.

Chakras are the 7 sources of divine power contained in growing human body. Such centers of energy each reflect an appropriate state of consciousness inside a person and control their psychological status and also the relation to the metaphysical and physical world. Visually shown as spinning wheels down the body centre, they derive from The Vedas. Birth of the chakravartin known as the chariot wheel or chakra is explained by these ancient Indian texts.

The force, called the "chi" comes into the crowns chakra from the universe. From there, every chakra is passed down, bringing fresh life and healing through purification of the troublesome emotions and eliminating the associated negative energy. The energy reverses and travels up at the bodies root chakra and is flowing out through the crown, entering the universe again.

Even if one chakra point is too small or too big, they won't allow the force to properly transfer through them, so that the person's soul won't be able to develop in understanding and maturity until they solve their problem of chakra imbalance. Its balance is a product of a body that is healthy. Similar to an ecosystem that functions symbiotically to preserve harmonic equilibrium at all levels, the body should do this also. When one body organ or chakra is not balanced or does not function at its best, over time, the harmony of the other parts of the body may be drastically affected. The mismatch results in illness and other problems.

The position of the root chakra is at the spine's base or coccyx's tip, and from there, the root chakra is linked to the part of earth, which gives the body a feeling of balance, equilibrium, strength, and grounding – providing a feeling of security.

Root chakra which has sluggish vibrations and gestures is closely related to Crown chakra. Those two maintain a control in body hormones. It's important to remember if one is a little imbalanced, the work of both is compromised.

The root chakra is also connected to the body's bones, such as nails, teeth etc. In addition, the rook chakra is often connected to the prostate, gonads, colon, anus and especially the adrenal glands. We must remember that in humans the adrenal gland is a very vital, primary and critical organ, as it plays an essential role in the production of cortisol related to survival. As we know, the cortisol stimulates the fight or flight reaction. Also the adrenal glands have a connection with third chakra indicated by flooring energy into the body.

A rising negative attribute of root chakra is fear. Fear can be a big problem it becomes unstable. Fears of becoming mentally and physically lost, reluctance to move on, reluctance to change, and a reluctance to accept oneself or difficulty. Positive thoughts and behavior must build up one's confidence. You should begin by expressing emotions of appreciation, using mantras of "self-love," establishing targets, and performing random kindness may help to relax your root chakra and to minimize the sense of anxiety.

One way of looking at illness's physiology is through the body's seven chakras. The seven chakras comprise:

6.1 The Root Chakra

If ones root chakra is closed too much, it may lead to the following issues:

- the individual will grow and develop into a complex person
- the complex person will always be worrisome about wealth
- the individual will be lost because of poor satisfaction about his life and status
- the individual will, as a result, be very pessimistic about his future

That may result in behavior that is very addictive self-destructive.

Root chakra being too open can cause the emotion of isolation and loneliness, unable to connect with the surrounding world. This may result in an urge for selfishness material possession and loveless attitude.

6.2 The Sacral Chakra

If the sacral chakra is too closed, then a lack of harmony in one's life is produced. As a result, one enjoy what they enjoy in life; they withdraw and become reclusive from social circumstances, friends, and family. Instead, they are unwilling to pay attention to themselves and work to help others whilst giving their desires no priority.

When the sacral chakra becomes too open, addictive habits, mistreatment, coercion, fear of loss can all turn into problems. To such an individual, the practice of calming massages, meditation, reflexology, and aromatherapy on sacral chakra dependent organs is quite beneficial. Since the chakra aspect is water, one should take hot baths mixed with mandarin or orange essential oils, or relax in a spa.

6.3 Solar Plexus Chakra

After you start to carry consciousness to the solar plexus, you resurface and awaken pushed back feelings like anger, pain, or terror. It is necessary to address these problems in order to restore peace to your body and chakra as whole.

The person is more likely to experience lots of frustration if the solar plexus becomes too open – they can push this down. The more someone suppresses their emotions, the more the chakra becomes unbalanced, and the body along with it. This can contribute to low self-esteem, loss of trust, lack of independence, little interest in life, low encouragement, and a lower overall worth and self-image. This may even cause poor digestion, potential ulcers, hepatitis, and IBS, too.

One easy way to bring your solar plexus back into balance is by cleaning the body and improving digestion. That can be accomplished by qigong exercise, jogging. In addition to strength, walking also helps to feel the vitality of your Chakra.

Carrying stones with yourself can also help boost and align the solar plexus chakra properly. These include and are not limited to; tiger eye, amber, yellow jasper, yellow citrine, topaz etc.

6.4 Heart Chakra

The Chakra of the heart is about loving yourself. It is without constraint, connecting, love and healing. It is a fast and relaxing chakra located in the chest or heart which causes the body to move continuously. This has a significant effect on the body as it is air related; to the heart, upper back, sternum, lungs, circulation of oxygen and blood. Such parts may be affected if the Chakra presents an imbalance. This is a very essential chakras for the body, since it preserves the order for the other chakras. This is because three chakras right above the heart and three are below that chakra. Therefore this renders the core a center for converging forces.

The right of the heart chakra is love, and when the child is in the early stages of his life, that is, between age three and age seven, it is fully established in the body. This makes it very important to show the children affection and compassion as they age. A depressive characteristic of heart chakra is grief. We don't feel secure with the idea that something may happen according to plan and the heart chakra is skewed or unbalanced, that may contribute to a lot of sadness. When left untreated, this can result in permanent depression. Loving is important for the chakra to soften and to grieve. The unbalanced core chakra correlates with body conditions like asthma, allergy, influenza, and heart failure. One is concerned about their emotional comfort, and has problems with compassion and acceptance of themselves. Knowledge of this is required to add peace to the heart chakra once again. Much of the suffering, sadness, loss accumulated in the heart is released with a gentle ease and determination. Heart chakra provides lots of love, however in return it also needs love, so it is important to put yourself with people who are caring, loving and optimistic to keep the chakra of the heart in equilibrium. The more relaxed the chakra is, the simpler a love and laugh would be. It is also been demonstrated that Laughter is effective against high pressure in blood. Although calming the circulatory system and the lungs, Qigong also tends to calm heart chakra. Exercising this feeling through physical contact and massage is very important because touch is also associated with the heart chakra. The contact provides positive guidance, ensuring that all actions are performed intentionally and with affection. Holding stones like rose quartz, jade, aventurine, tourmaline, emeralds, and moss agate is often helpful.

6.5 The Throat Chakra

The chakra of the throat is very much about expressing yourself, communicating, motivation, imagination and feelings. It has right to talk, and to be understood. This chakra on the throat is connected to the element of space or ether. This Chakra is in the chest. This chakra is often fast and requires space or room to move inside the shape. If there's no room, however, there'll be no shape. At throat chakra; arm, parathyroid gland, mouth, windpipe, thyroid, and upper lung have a strong effect. The main guiding factor is durability. To use one's speech is to the right of the throat chakra. Its bodily production typically occurs when an individual is between the age of seven to twelve. That fact makes it necessary to allow children to make their own thoughts, be heard, and to express in an atmosphere of support and caring. The significant negative characteristics of the chakra throat are deceit, dishonesty, and loss of modesty. On the opposite, when the chakra is distorted or pushed down, it may result in an individual not hearing their speech. It can, however, lead to their being dishonest to others, along with being unable to communicate thoughts and feelings. If the throat chakra is irritated, the throat may start to feel blocked, warm, itchy, or even a little tickle on the back. If it gets very serious it can lead to thyroid problems, time-keeping problems, hearing impairment, and problem in sense of time. Moreover, if the chakra is unstable or in excess, the chakra will become very troublesome because one cannot do justice to oneself, they can't stand up for their own self and allow themselves to get pushed down. Another important fact is that one may not be able to articulate oneself properly with excess in the throat chakra; such a person will hardly ever, avoid listening to other people's advice, and can become extremely prejudiced and unwilling to consider and listen to others' opinions. Working toward acceptance, self-esteem, and compassion for others will continue a helpful healing process for the chakra of the throat.

To continue to relax the throat chakra, one may hit gently with one's hands on one's chest, humming slowly, singing like a mantra; I will convey my real self and thereby engage completely in my own trend. (Or) I welcome and accept transition. Concentrate on your imagination and communication, attend a dance class, read poetry or join an art class. Such an atmosphere should foster your creativity, improve your communication and help to properly work them out. It loosens the face and releases tension in the jaw and mouth. Also, Qiigong facial massage is very effective in calming and reinforcing the chakra in the throat. Meditation also works well to open the heart chakra, like Halasana / Matsyasana, shoulder stand pose, and meditation-yoga mantra, and chanting. The cure cycle functions by holding gemstones like apatite, turquoise, angelite, aquamarine, blue lace agate etc.

6.6 Third Eye Chakra

Also called brow chakra, it is about sovereignty. It keeps the moral code of soul, mind and body, and tells what's right and wrong. It lets us see something our eyes cannot outwardly perceive.

Typically it is on the forehead or between the lips. The third eye is swifter, works faster in the mouth than the chakra. It carries a substantial effect on the forehead, brain, sinuses, eyes, ears, nose, pituitary gland, central nervous system, and face.

True energy and awareness of all things on earth are correlated with the third eye of the mind. It gives us intuition and insight. When the mind's eye is open fully, it retains all of its ability to discern truth from the facts and to offer wisdom.

Illusion is a negative-dominant dimension to the chakra of the third-eye. There are a lot of things in the universe which may amaze us. We must however be able to view them for what they really are. Third eye helps the person to differentiate between the false perceptions when optimally operating. This will encourage people to start doing what is morally right as they'll be equipped with insight and intuition when they see it — to perceive the surrounding world more accurately, to know what's best for themselves.

The third eye when out of control, can make you experience problems in vision, hallucinations and headaches. It may be that you often wrong life decisions and blind your eyes to reality. To activate the chara of the third eye, it is vital to find the middle of the forehead and reflect on the mind's eye, sense the rhythm and his presence. Think how it travels to and fro through the base of foot and through the world in the centre of the brain to visualize. In some time to imagine that it is in your mind.

Meditating is a good process to bring concentration and connection to the chakra of third eye. Carrying stones on you will allow opening of the third eye. The stones include; star sapphire, quartz, lazuri and lapis.

6.7 The Crown Chakra

The crown chakra is about understanding yourself and the greater purpose of one's life. The sign is a connection of thought and of divinity. The right is to learn, and crown chakra grows your entire life and evolves. Usually, the crown chakra is found on above your head, the cerebral cortex or central nervous system. It extends continuously up above towards the universe. Crown chakra is closely related to the pituitary gland and the cerebrum. Crown chakra is a synonym for a full blend of the soul and a genuine self-knowledge. It gives us true knowledge, and the opportunity to surrender yourself and serve a higher force or strength in the universe. From this crown chakra radiate the colors white, purple and violet. A dominant-negative trait of the crown chakra is attachment. This is often the case when one is recklessly committed to another someone or material object when depression, loneliness, boredom, inability to focus or learn, and uncertainty can become dominant in their lives. When you continue to back away from what you really need to be doing in your life, you stop the bond between the crowns and the universe and therefore lack a contact with your body. A poor crown chakra may trigger an individual in their lives to cultivate much phobia and fear. They are helpless without trusting on their skill to live their lives, and turn to physical things to add purpose and meaning to their lives. That leaves one too unable to experience life's other wonders and pleasures. Feeling the pleasures of life along with understanding what its fundamental nature is, is essential. In order to carry responsiveness to the chakra of crown one should grow their confidence coupled with a trust in the greater meaning of life. Another good way to boost the chakra on the crown is by contemplation on crystals. By placing gemstones such as howlite, quartz, diamond, amethyst, labradorite above your head as you meditate, the crown chakra will open and get stronger. This also helps build, purify, and leave a pure spirit inside the body.

Chapter 7: Reiki Hand Positions and Levels

Ever entered a space and felt uncomfortable, without some fair answer, why? Have you ever worried of someone randomly, just to hear from them shortly after?

Every arising matter emanates from an electric field (aura). A forest has an aura, a novel has an aura and you do have an aura. In the aforementioned examples, you involuntarily sense and interact with another's auras. This force field remains beyond the spectrum of our regular vision but it can be sensed by all of those who have intuitive abilities. The chakras are the force centres inside the aura. The energy field has seven main chakras, each covering certain aspects of your life (such as culture, health care, education, self-confidence, imagination, relationships ...). They take energy from the fundamental force of existence which is necessary for the healthy functioning of the own system. When a chakra will not work correctly, it can influence your life. Throughout the outward physical truth, disease and disharmony eventually manifest when chakras become out of balance, blocked or exhausted. Any problem you find in your outer life has begun off as an internal energy blockage. Each issue you find in your outer life has begun out as an aggressive internal question. The condition of your energy environment, basically, defines your reality. You don't have to focus on the stuff of your life that don't suit. You need to concentrate on looking after your field of energy. Changing your energy field makes your life turn around. The awareness is not fresh. This awareness has been a part of many societies throughout history; it is only new to us in today's western world. You can only solve problems within your energy field at the start. The Reiki cleans and enhances the chakras, helping them to function to their maximum capacity. The cure removes blockages and helps the force field vibrate. The Reiki cleans the chakras and enhances them, enabling them to function to their maximum capacity. The cure removes blockages and raises activity in the energy field.

7.1 Reiki Hand Positions

Given below is the description of Reiki Hand positions:
POSITION 1 – FACE

For yourself– The palms of your hands are placed against your face. The hands are gently cupped over your eyes and on your foreheads. Note, you needn't exert pressure on your face, only tap it gently.

For others– Place your hands on their faces, softly resting palms on their foreheads while cupping your hands around their lips.

POSITION 2–TOP OF HEAD AND CROWN

For yourself– Hands are placed on both sides of the head with the hands' palms lying near the ears, and the fingertips touching the crown of the head.

For others–put the hands around their head, rubbing the inner wrists and covering the ears with the fingertips.

POSITION 3–BACK OF HEAD

For yourself– Hands are placed with one at the back of the heads and one at the nape of the neck.

For others– Tuck the hands beneath their head gently, making a nest for them to rest their heads in. Let the back of the hands rest on a table or pillow.

Place 4–JAWLINE AND CHIN

For yourself– The chin lies in the palms of your cupped hands, so you can curl your hands around the jaw line.

For others– Surround the jaw line with your hands, letting your fingertips to brush under their chin when your hands' heels rest softly over or close to the ears.

POSITION 5–HEART, NECK AND COLLARBONE

For yourself– One hand grabs the neck gently, the neck rests comfortably inside the V shaped by the thumb and forefinger, whereas the other hand rests between the center of the heart and the collarbone.

For Others – Place the right hand really softly around their face. When they don't get satisfied with this hand positioning, you may instead let your hand float over the spot. Put your left hand over your heart core.

POSITION 6–RIB CAGE AND RIBS

For yourself–Hands are placed just below the breast on the upper rib cage.

For others–Position hands just below the breasts on the upper rib cage. One hand will go out in front of the other.

POSITION 7–ABDOMEN

For yourself–Hands are positioned on the area of the solar plexus just above the navel with fingertips touching.

For others- Hands are placed just above the navel on their solar plexus region. One hand will go out in front of the other.

Place 8–PELVIC BONES

For yourself–Each hand is positioned on each pelvic bone with fingertips touching.

For others–Each hand is positioned on each pelvic bone. One hand will go out in front of the other.

POSITION 9–SHOULDER BLADES

For Yourself- Hands are put on shoulder blades. When you are having a session yourself and can't reach that far behind you, you should place your hands on top of each arm instead.

For Others – Make them to lie on their bellies. Hands are placed on the shoulder blades, the position that houses other emotional stresses. This is an environment that you may need to handle for a little longer to better move the energies than most do.

POSITION 10-MID-BACK

For Yourself- The hands are positioned in the back centre.

For Others-- Hands are put in the back core. One side will move out in front of the other.

POSITION 11–LOWER BACK

For Yourself-Place your hands on the lower back.

For Others–You can easily move your hands down the back and position them over the lower back section. One hand will go out in front of the other.

POSITION 12–SACRUM

For yourself–Hands are placed at the top of the buttocks, on the sacral region of the body.

For Others–Follow the same protocol as you administer for yourself.

Levels/Degrees of Reiki

Usui Sensei divided the Reiki program into three different degrees or stages of instruction.

Every degree is established at the initial learning stage and thus helps the student to develop within it. Whoever religion or political beliefs, in Reiki everyone will get instruction.

7.2 First Degree – Reiki Level 1 (Shoden)

Shoden is a Japanese word indicating the first lessons.' This is usually the first training step of the mainstream Reiki division of Japan. This is also known as Usui Reiki Ryoho.Shoden-Reiki Level 1 offers meditation techniques to reinforce and relax your mind, gives a clearer understanding of how mind works in your existence and its effects, fosters a divine attachment to existence that helps you feel healthier and secure, furnishes you with the ability to cure yourself and others by putting your hands on or around your body.

Learn from a Reiki Master the Common Way for Learning Reiki Level 1

You should ask for a recommendation from someone particularly if that individual has studied Reiki himself. If not, search for Reiki Connections at your country of residence. Typically they maintain lists of qualified Reiki masters and you can locate one near you.

You may begin by opting for a course on Reiki or Reiki therapy in your quest for Reiki masters and their evaluation. Not only can this be good for your health and general well-being, it would also serve to gage the ability level of the prospective Reiki instructor. You'll still be able to determine your comfort level with the instructor and his lessons through the process.

Tell for their origins, as well. Reiki is like a family tree that can be tracked back to Reiki initial master practitioner. For starters, Reiki Western training will take you back to Mikao Usui, Chjiro Hayashi or Hawayo Takata. Note also that one of the 22 masters she taught in Reiki should have the lineages leading to Hawayo Takata.

Through Reiki the way certain forms of treatment are learned is usually not observed and studied. It is handed on from the Reiki Master to the client during an attunement process. This process opens the crown, heart, and palm chakras and establishes a special bond between the receiver and the Reiki source. The Reiki tuning is a strong healing activity. The Attunement Energies are channeled through the student by the Master of Reiki. The approach is guided by the Rei or God-consciousness, and improvements to the system are made according to the needs of each pupil. Reiki guides and other heavenly powers also assist in initiating the attunement communication process. Some document divine events from a previous life including personal messages, healings, dreams, and encounters. The tuning may also improve psychological sensitivity. Students often report observations involving: third-eye raising, enhanced emotional awareness, and other spiritual abilities after a Reiki tuning is received.

Preparing for Attunement

It's suggested to use a purification technique to boost the performance you receive during the tuning. This will allow the Attunement Energies to work more efficiently and offer you greater benefits. The steps to take in its series are discretionary and not compulsory. If you are motivated to do so, then stick to it.

1. Refrain from eating meat, fowl, or fish three days previous to the settlement. Such foods also contain penicillin and female hormones, and contaminants in the form of pesticides and heavy metals which slow down your body and throw it out of control.

2. Consider a fast of one to three days of water or juice, particularly if you are already a vegetarian or are experiencing fasting.

3. Minimize or completely stop consuming coffee and caffeine drinks. We develop imbalances in the nerves and endocrines. Do not use any caffeine drinks during the attunement day.

4. Shall not use alcohol at least three days in preparation of the tuning.

5. Reduce candy, or prohibit them.

6. Cut back on the day of tuning while you drink, just consume as little as possible.

7. Meditate an hour a day using a method you're comfortable with, or actually invest this period in solitude for at least a week.

8. Reduce or reduce the amount of time you waste viewing Television, listening to the radio and reading newspapers.

9. Go for peaceful hikes, spend time with nature, and work out in moderation.

10. Pay heed to the feelings and unconscious experiences inside and outside. Contemplate the significance and awareness of certain things that affect you.

11. Seek to release all rage, terror, envy, hate and anxiety. Focus on creating a sacred space within yourself and around you.

12. You will become part of a community of people who use Reiki to heal themselves and each other and who work together to heal the world by being in harmony with each other.

Procedure and Duration of Reiki

In a level 1 Reiki attunement, students are tuned to three separate icons, each representing a specific dimension of Reiki energy: power, mental / emotional balance and distance healing. In four separate stages and periods each student receives tunings to these three symbols. The relation fortifies and deepens with growing repetition.

This is usually offered over a 1-2 day time span.

Reiki Level 1 Lesson-Learning about Reiki

You will learn about Reiki, Reiki history and how Reiki works during the teaching process and gain knowledge on it. The course requires a manual or print-out that incorporates the course material. If not, please try to take notes after the lesson. After the course several Reiki Masters are eligible for follow-up questions or consultations.

Reiki Level 1 Lesson-Attunement

A Reiki Level 1 Attunement is simply a technique that sets you to the Reiki energy frequency so you can funnel Reiki energy through yourself and others. The Attunement is a type of ritual which is held hidden by the Reiki master. The Reiki master will rely for students to hold their eyes closed during the process. Closed eyes allow the Attunement interaction inward attention smoother and caring. The master of Reiki makes use of a combination of icons and mantras to connect you to Reiki's common life power.

Reiki Level 1 Lesson–Practice

You'll experience a lot of anticipation heading up to the Attunement, and while it's a relaxing phase it's also a relief when it's over. The rehearsal stage becomes more relaxed and fun to do. So this will allow you the chance to feel Reiki energies for the first time.

The practitioner will offer Reiki meditations which are helpful to strengthen and maintain the Reiki wave.

Channeling the Reiki force has a remarkable similarity to a water stream or tube. If they are not used for a while the pipe blocks, limiting the flow. The meditations, coupled with regular use of Reiki, help restrict the said and encourage energy channeling.

Benefits of Shoden

- Learn how to relax
- Gain a good understanding of energy work
- Experience emotional and physical release
- Feel relaxed with yourself
- Cultivate your caring and loving qualities
- Support others
- Feel secure
- Be acquainted with the Reiki method
- Receive ongoing individual care and encouragement from your instructor
- Belong to an international group of healers

Reiki's First Degree is a really gentle and life-changing introduction to Reiki's strength. Usui usually instructed his first stage students how to self-heal. Reiki 1 is arranged the way Usui has been doing. Students are given four 'attunements' from a Reiki Master, which aligns the student with the Reiki energy and helps them transmit Reiki to themselves and family and friends. During this first step of study,

students are introduced to the Precepts, and inspired to live by them. There are also some energy activities displayed which they are expected to perform on a regular basis. There is introduced the energy centers of the body, called Chakras, and their significance is taught at this point of the healing cycle. Additionally, the practice of mindfulness is learned at this level, because this element of teaching is so important for the student's continued progress. The first degree is delivered over a two-day period during which the pupil will be able to conduct himself easily with Reiki as well as with family and friends. Reiki 1 is the beginning of several positive changes for the students as they continue on many levels to restore their own lives. All who may want to develop more should do so by learning the next Reiki degree, allowing a period of three months between the Reiki stages hopefully.

The environments for Reiki Level 2 and Reiki Master are close in design, but they include different icons, each with a specific purpose to unlock the energy pathways.

7.3 Second Degree – Reiki Level 2 (Okuden)

The second degree of Reiki is called a Western Practitioner Standard. Students obtain two extra attunements from a Reiki Master at the teaching level, and then elevates their sensation to a greater degree. As a Reiki practitioner, the emphasis is now on more self-healing and development as well as supporting others. The Chakras (energy centers) deepening is taught, and students are shown how to feel the variations in electricity. It then lets them examine a person's body before a Reiki treatment is provided. Reiki icons are added, and before doing certain procedures, students are taught how to use them, through their attention and intent. Students are encouraged to start using their intuition and healing purpose, and rely more on it at this stage. The Reiki energy still understands what it is doing and where to go, so when left to function on an unconscious level, it is really straightforward to transfer the energy to the students. Distance healing is often taught at this point, and students are encouraged to use this healing method both to enhance their own lives and to assist the world and all those who live within.

Students will also learn how to set up a Reiki practice because in the West, Reiki 2 is considered to be a skilled qualification. It includes training students how to take strong background information from friends, use outstanding communication and comprehension abilities, and also how to use it as expertise and store it as it is. Honesty and anonymity are extremely essential to any Reiki practitioner and this is always learned throughout the method. Other areas include buying adequate equipment, insurance and meaningful advertising. Students are often taught the value of both physically, mentally, and spiritually as well as energetically supporting themselves.

Third Degree–Reiki Level 3/Master (Shinpiden)

The third degree in Reiki allows the student to become a Reiki Master for a span of time. The degree is taught in two sections as well. The student is a Reiki Master in the first section, and the second is where the student begins to practice Reiki, and thereby becomes a Reiki Master Teacher. During this level , students are attuned to the Master level which is a very powerful and beautiful attunement. It, again, raises the student's relaxation surge to an even greater degree and improves the Reiki skills gained beforehand. Students are taught the Master's words, which will then be included in the attunement cycle to others whenever the subject determines they wish to instruct. Throughout this level, in addition to more activities on strength, meditation as a activity is taught positively. This degree is about expanding the perception of the Reiki energy, being more intentionally sensitive, fostering more insight, and actively acting with purpose. Observing Reiki lessons is essential to becoming a Reiki Master Instructor, coupled with a clear knowledge of training methods and learning. To become a Master of Reiki is just another step down the road to spiritual development. The Reiki energy helps personal growth and trust to begin, and can continually change and enrich your life. The resources are starting to increase at this level and studying is becoming a much deeper activity. Level 3 in Reiki is about self-mastery that we all cannot happen overnight! This is a cycle of living and learning but it comes from an inner power role. Everything is more necessary to realize who you are and to have a career of concentrating on whom you aspire to be. It's about staying true to yourself, unconditionally enjoying yourself and following your innate gifts and strengths in this world while serving the supreme goal. The Masteries we are concerned about here are devotion, empathy, kindness, humility and acceptance. Self-mastery puts you at the center of your life-driver. Not only are you the joyful rider on a joyous trip, but you create the future you desire by your feelings, desires, decisions and practice. You are no longer a life victim but a powerful life-maker you want. So Breathe – it might sound like a big struggle but note that with love and empathy we come home. Every day we wish to perform positive and charitable actions. Training is a means to remind oneself to remember letting go, to remember getting back, to remember – at Reiki Master Point, we 're not finished with Reiki. We've come in full circle, instead. We arrive at the beginning yet again – the easy laying on of hands to oneself.

Chapter 8: Balancing and Healing Of Chakras with Reiki Guided Meditation

Reiki Meditations is an essential experience for all those who wish to cultivate daily happiness and inner peace. Every morning and every evening Mikao Usui stressed a lot much to ponder on. Driven meditation promotes slipping quite comfortably and rapidly into a profoundly relaxing state of mind. The tensed muscles and chattering mind calms down with controlled meditation, transmitting a profound sense of relaxation and harmony within oneself. Along with the calm led meditation, you can conduct Reiki therapy to cure and stabilize chakras. Using Meditation, Reiki, Love, and wisdom you can improve the quality of life. In the past 10 years, American perception of Reiki has significantly improved. Reiki has grown from a less known 'fresh age treatment' to a well-known popular and appreciated complementary technique, mostly used around the world in hospices and hospitals. But it's a lot more than a therapy of healing of course. Human development outside it won't bring the inside happiness and peace that we desire. How can it happen? How can the development of external bring results internally? Only inward development can produce results within. The inner virtues are pleasure, harmony, contentment, empathy, joy, compassion, and affection. They aren't made of stone, wood, or metal. Clearly the stuff we build outside makes our life a bit simpler and also offers great value. We just require hospitals, roads, schools, etc. Such issues are important for the functioning of the modern world. Suffering can be reduced by them and improve our standard of living. Still, in these stuff, we will never consider a 'final answer. When we spend so much energy socially building what happens to the inner world of ours? It just degenerates. The inner values become poorer and poorer as we prioritize external growth over internal progress. More concerned we are becoming with our welfare, more suspect, more discriminating, less patient, less content, and less kind. Our impulses are growing, so more external stimulation is required to fulfill our childlike mind. An individual with considerable insight may not need to see an insistence on external growth will inevitably put this planet to end. The purpose of meditation is inner creation. We are just being alone. We aren't outer creatures of course; we only forget our existence. We are so wrapped in the outside world and we forget what it is to be a spiritual being, we forget who are we. It's almost like we've fallen under some spell and still feel we should pursue peace 'outside.' If we have all right 'in,' the required career, the right wife, the right car that we'll be satisfied with. Of example, just 'within' will be found the feeling of joy and satisfaction we try in outward things. We ought to search inwards. There is no significant sign of what we do outwardly in our life. Once the life of ours comes to the end we will be removed from all belongings and persons. We just ought to pass that. Death is inevitable and we're going to have to leave it. Life passes fast too, not even 70-80 years is a lengthy time. Ask anyone who is retired, and they'll say that you don't have time for wasting and making the best of life is vital. Every day talking about this lets one concentrate on what's important, and leave what's not essential. When we die, we cannot take anything with us, except our qualities within. Becoming an inner self, someone that wants to develop his/her inside qualities is so important for that.

Reiki will help us transform internally particularly when paired with Buddhist wisdom and meditation. It will encourage us to become inward beings and slowly relinquish our need for outer growth and transient enjoyment. This is a great voyage to get started. Self-discovery is a road. It's a true life trip. It's about knowing what life really entails. Our inner existence is our true life, it's when we decide to look inward that the life of ours truly starts. This truly is our celebration!

8.1 Preparatory steps before Meditation

Practice the steps referred to below use background soft music for calming purpose.

1. Find a quiet place to go through meditation, and a comfortable position.

2. Bring in the Reiki Healing Masters, the Guardian Angels, Archangel Michael and all other celestial spirits whom you might want to be near you.

3. Demand Archangel Michael to drive out all disruptive or trapped energies from the room surrounding you. Tell him to cover your aura in a violet light bubble, and the room surrounding you.

4. Trigger on both palms the Reiki symbols with the purpose of curing and calming chakras – Dai Ko Myo (If tuned to Master Symbol), Hon Sha Zi Sho Nen, Sei He Ki and Cho Ku Rei.

8.2 The Meditation Stages

The meditations can be divide into the following five stages:

Posture establishment

Intention establishment

The meditation body

The phase of dissolving

The merit sharing.

At these phases, we will look now stage by stage.

Posture establishment

The meditation space should be prepared by us before we commence the meditation. This includes the setting up of our cushion or chair for meditation and makes sure that members of the family do not disturb our session; including pets. We should bear in mind switching off the cell phones and setting our phone to silent mode or from socket simply unplugging it.

Once we set up around space we set up a sound meditation postures. Attending the seven posture points * (including the head; hands; arm; legs back; eyes; jaw; and tongue) we prepare ourselves for following the meditation, both mentally and physically.

Intention establishment

The 2nd stage is to determine what we plan to do. Before starting the meditation it's vital to state every meditation we would like to continue. Intention setting also means cultivating the correct motivation to do the practice of meditation. The 4 contemplations are a perfect means of creating the correct inspiration. We will do so for the correct purposes while we meditate and the purpose is to help others. Those four reflections inspire one to meditate. Talking about this is helpful, and raising the question that "Why meditation is chosen by me and what do I want to learn from meditation?"The better we will find our work incentive the sooner we can reap the gain of doing so. Most especially we will consider that not just for our sake only but for benefiting of all life we do our meditation practice. If from a place we come where the positive is exchanged with everyone, it makes one develop the diversity of mind. In the cycle of clear recognition where we say, "like the Buddha, we act before we are a Buddha" and we (finally) become one. This is regarded as Bodhichitta cultivation In Buddhism that converts into the generation of consciousness towards enlightenment. Bodhichitta contains the desire to be an enlightened person with the utmost of empathy and kindness, to benefit others. For first it may be hard to truly understand this sensation of kindness and love toward all people, so maybe it's better to start with those to whom we 're near to, us like our families, colleagues, loved ones, kids, and our pets even. When we have developed this Bodhichitta mentality, it is simpler to apply the feeling of kindness and love to the 'tough customers' we meet in life. That is a practice of meditation in itself. No matter how we select for generating our motivation and intention, this must be completed before the start of our session of meditation. Just like embarking on some journey to someplace, we have never been, setting up a good motivation is similar to roadmap checking and getting to understand how that destination can be achieved in the most carefree, simple, and beneficial way possible.

The Meditation Body

Once our intention is established, we calm the mind of ours by being aware at the tip of our noses of breath, coming & going, and letting go of all the feelings and thoughts.

Catching the air lets one keep the mind intact in one position. Once we've silenced the mind we're bringing out something beneficial of this place. They also align and harmonize the inside and outside energies within the body by breath consciousness

Form this position the meditation body starts. We've spent the most time in this 3rd phase and hopefully attaining the rewards, greatest one. Whether on a specific mudra we're meditating or engaged in some meditation that includes seeing strength and illumination, we can also keep in mind that we're here, and when finally we find that the mind of ours has 'leave the room' we are continually taking ourselves back to the actual activity.

What's not helpful is thinking: "Oh no, I missed it once again," but then actually get the attention again to the training topic and move on.

It's like to be present at a railway station, the busy one when thoughts come and go. We see trains coming in and stopping at the platform. Then we see the onboard passengers and after that, we see the leaving trains. Attending our meditation means noticing that the trains are coming and then going instead of jumping and go on a trip. If or maybe I must say 'when' we notice we've hopped on some train, we must bring our self-back to peace & mindfulness station and continue with that practice

Based on the mediation exercise you're doing that can often include a process of building up where we create energy forms and from space, light out or visualize energy flows in our body throughout. This activity additional phase is where we start to interact according to the particular practice, with energy forms and light. Whenever we go for these meditations it's necessary to remove such visualizations that I'll discuss in the section below.

The Phase of Dissolving

Several meditations do have a phase of dissolution. The meaning of this is that anything that in mind is produced or imagined is put back in mind. It's not usual for us to leave what we've created out in the space in action

After a long trip, we should think of the phase of dissolving such as packing the luggage. When we go from the hotel and we do not leave around with all the stuff, we pack them neatly and cleanly and take along with us our bag. It's about adding a sign at the letter's end, then reminding at the sentence end to compose our complete stops.

When in a phase of dissolution we engage ourselves everything is mixed by us that we were produced in the mind back to us or ourselves. By this, it is recognized by us that it isn't a thing that is fixed or permanent, nor it's something that resides outside of ourselves, but it is something that has emerged from the unlimited potential of ours and is thus self-empowering and self-reliance it cultivates.

The Merit Sharing

We generate certain positive energy each time meditation is completed by us. Given our meditation's expected outcomes some positive has resulted simply by this doing. The explanation for this because meditation is a special practice, so we can produce beneficial energy inside our body so atmosphere by merely participating in meditation.

If you've got something better then you are not sharing it why? When the merit is dictated by us, we believe that whatever peace of joy and mind happiness generated by the result of meditation, it will not be shared for our welfare only, but the welfare of all life.

This dedication might be chosen by us in a sense generally, or if someone known by us is there that can benefit really, or someone in help, there can be thought by us that all the generated merit by this practice is shared now for the concerned person.

When the merit is started for another, a wish by us that they recover or be healthy or that as a result of the meditation, positive energy might be received by them. Merit sharing is like making other's wishes. It empowers also life-energy of ours when sharing this intent. We do so because we know we're one and many are there.

Selling the value often evokes a kindness feeling and cooperation. As a consequence, we continue infinitely seeing the universe, full of opportunity and plentiful.

8.3 Let's Start

Step-wise practicing of Reiki meditation is given below:

Step One

Start inhaling slowly at the 4th count and in one go release the breath through the mouth. Repeat it one time more and relax.

Step Two

When you count from five to one, the body can begin to expel all the tension and ache in the muscles stored and fall into a truly serene and calm state.

At the count of 5

Your foot, toe, knee & calf muscles should be loose

At the count of 4

Your lower back, thigh & pelvis muscles feel relaxed

At the count of 3

Your chest, abdominal, hands & shoulders muscles feel relaxed

At the count of 2

Your facial, neck and upper back muscles should be loose

And At the count of 1

Your hair follicles and scalp muscles feel relaxed

Step Three

Now at the time of sunrise visualize that you are having a walk on a seashore. The cool fresh air at the shore you breathe is immensely rejuvenating and refreshing. For sitting a comfortable place is found by you while you walk along this beautiful shore. You turn up as you look at the Sun steadily working its way by passing through the cloud cover to greet the earth and you. In your sleep and appearance on the beach, the sun is the protection and guardian of you.

Do the chakra healing exercise below for as long as you like each chakra to recover like 4 to 5 minutes or more and now then go on to the next one chakra.

Step Four

The highest-dimensional Reiki force now passes into the Root Chakra of yours to cure, coordinate, and even it out. See that the Red Color-filled waves are gushing onto the sea, sweeping out from inside out, the Root Chakra.

Follow Solar Plexus, Sacral, Lung, Throat, Third Finger, and Chakra of Crown directions as set out above.

Step Five

Visualize the roots that emerge from the foot and reach 10-15 feet down into Mother Earth. The energy of Reiki now will flow through the chakra of your foot, sending all the build-up and excess energy from the body into Mother Earth for grounding the energy field.

Step Six

You have to thank you Reiki Energy Masters, Archangel Michael, Divine Sun, and Guardian Angels for your healing. See yourself inside a Blue light security sphere.

8.4 Reiki Guided Meditation for Group Healing

This is a guided meditation intended for use as a warm up by R or meditation groups, a preliminary group meditation meant to put everyone in a protected and grounded, relaxed, open state. It features a beautiful visualization of a stream and it's cleaning healing powers and then proceeds to a chakra cleaning and opening meditation involving a waterfall's changing colors. You can start by making it sure that all of you sit comfortably with your feet on the ground firmly and straight on our backs. When we start our deep breathing, raise your shoulders, and after that drop the shoulders and gently part the mouth to let the air exhale. Close your head. Rest your hands in the lap. Sure, you are feeling wet. To keep yourself warm during meditation, wrap a blanket around you if you want. Focus now on breathing and inhaling through the nose and take a breath deeply starting from our diaphragm and also be aware of the air filling your lungs and resulting in the abdomen expanding and rising. When no longer you can inhale, simply hold for some secs and then release the breath gently, very gently. Think of a white stream of energy reaching the crown chakra when you inhale, then filling every single cell inside the body with luminescent white light. And during exhale, you release any tension in the body that might exist, release any tension, stress, pain. You just allow it to go all. So with "in" breath, healing, renewing, invigorating, and "out" breath comes in source energy. Remove concerns, remove doubts, and release unpleasant feelings of some sort. You imagine now roots going deep inside the earth from your feet and spreading out in a thousand tinier roots. These white roots go deep inside the earth, past rocks, crystals, deep down into the earth's beating heart, the core molten, in Mother Earth, The Spirit of Gaia. Pretty grounded you feel. You sound anchored. You feel safe and linked. Now imagine wrapped in a safe blanket around yourself. With its Teflon coating, that protects you. You are completely safe so that you are kept in love, protection, and light at every time as you connect with the spirit world, and communicate only with the purest and highest of spirits, ascend masters, and life forms. Imagine now that by slowly moving stream you are that winds way of it's through the beautiful countryside, lush dense. You go near the stream and now watch in the slow current, the aquatic plants and reeds gently undulating. Fish can be seen swimming inside the river. The water's sound is soothing, relaxing. You can sense the heat beating you hard, burning you up to the heart. You can also hear their pretty birdsong singing gently. You are serene and quiet. You wanted your toes to be dropped in the warm running stream, so inside warm water you drop your toes so glow and it looks like the river is massaging your hands and feet in the soft currents. You close the eyes of yours and just feel the sensation of flowing water and the sun that is warming your bodies and head and listening in their pretty song to the woodland birds. You feel the complete force of nature when you inhale and interact with all the living beings, plants, trees, birds, livestock, insects hills, and mountains. There is a feeling of universal connection and your Mother Earth grounded is strengthened. All your worries feel by you away flowing with the flux of stream, all your fears. The water cleanses you physically from all those doubts and concerns and unpleasant feelings. The feeling to let go and get free is liberating also. You find your hearts overflowing with affection for this magnificent world and all its marvelous sights, and all the incredible animals share the earth and you. It starts to burst and radiate outward as you fill yourself with the passion. You visualize this love interacting with the fellow meditators of yours, and when it interacts with your fellow meditators then it gets greater and starts to circulate through the community building with every revolution and when up to the great level it has grown, you take this love feeling up to the atmosphere just above the gravitational force of the planet and then it stays out of the world. It could be anyone you meet who needs help, it could be a place like Iraq or Syria where citizens live in terror and need the caring love. It could be an object which is endangered due to the acts of man. It may be a tree or plant which is endangered by the behavior of man. Guide the energy of loving down to the desired target and make it know the maximum power of the collective force of affection. Pick some other target and then energy is sent down again for subject bathe in the moist, caring, soothing light until you know your first target has experienced the maximum force of the energy of love healing. Now you are moving your focus out into the huge cosmos away from planet earth and reaching out with arms open and connecting with the universal energy. The past, current, and future are embraced by you and you give your love forward to any human person in million separate ways that may be present there in the huge universe. So you are trying to put the caring energy back into yourself and you are softly putting your hands over your hearts and taking back into yourself the beautiful calming spirit that has billions magnified times from being interacted with all the living creatures. You permit yourself to love, cherish, and nurture yourself. You sense the gentle waves of love divine energy flowing through you like the waves of pure rainwater, calming. Healing every of your chakras you sense the washed over water. Then, the water is packed with silver or white luminescence, light electricity, and you experience warm water relaxing, purifying, and opening the heart chakra fully. The water that is warm is now showering over you transforms color into a rich indigo hue, and you notice the third eye opening of yours and become alive fully and transparent. This energy of indigo triggered the maximum intuition and spiritual abilities. The water shifts to a dark purple blue again, and you sense the throat chakra expanding wide and all of the communicative skills are enabled to be completely exposed and awoken. You suddenly realize the water running through you is turning into a vivid green color and when this transition happens the chakra of the crown is opened and revitalized and you are overcome with love when you experience the complete force of the chakra of heart as the love runs over you. The water again changes into bright yellow sunshine and your solar chakra of plexus is enriched and awakened by wonderful water that flows and cascades over you. The heart of your being is this as is the sun in the

Solar System of ours. This awakens your trust, vitality, personal strength, and wellbeing. The chakra of solar plexus connects to many vital centers in your body, stomach, spleen, liver, gall bladder and so is important for your health. That powerful energy from the sun shines is feel by you from the solar plexus. To a bright orange color, the water shifts color again, like the sun falling in the west. You open the sacral chakra of your wide open to encourage it to release all its strength and capacity. That chakra is your body's emotional core, where all the emotions reside. Its creative power, ambition, dreams, emotions all live in here. So do the intimacy and passion. You feel wide opening up the full force of that chakra. And now the water gradually switches from an amber hue to a brilliant red the opening of the root chakra is feel by you and feeling motivated and powerful and alive. The chakra is this that roots you literally to the grounding of us on earth. It is the foundation upon which all is built. Your focus originates from a powerful root chakra. Start swaying in rhythm by you as there is a feeling of the root chakra open to the full. Now you will be bringing yourself back in the bodies. You must focus on the exercise. Take deep breaths that cover your mouth then gradually your breath is expelled. You are aware that your feet are ground touching firmly and sending deep the white roots into the core of the earth, grounding us up. You are well aware that you're safe lined Teflon blanket is always around you wrapped still keeping you in loving light and safety. You raise your eyes and move yourself some to get you straight back in the bodies.

Reiki Meditation Tips

Regular practice of Reiki's simple two-way meditation technique can't help only you in improving the focus of yours and spiritually awaken you but can also amplify the innate abilities of healing of yours to help in achieving the holistic health. Maintaining a very high-level energy of life force, Prana, holistic health prerequisite, achieved by various techniques practice that might results in generating a balance between the mind and body, like yoga, Reiki Quantum Touch, or Tai Chi, to name but a few. We both use one type of therapy or other as an essential component of physical, behavioral, and emotional care.

The Reiki 2-in-1 technique of meditation deftly combines both Reiki and meditation healing powers.

As a result of the synergy produced by mixing them together, the benefits accruing from them grow manifold. What keeps the meditation of Reiki apart from the other forms of meditation is the unique capacity of it's to reinforce the practitioner's capability of innate healing.

Mikao Usui resurrected the ancient practice of drawing energies for regeneration familiar as Reiki into the eternal life-force. Once a pupil asked him, "I have been practicing meditation for several years, why learning Reiki is needed for helping me learning the meditation?" Meditation an essential Reiki part. Usui observed that an essential component of his Reiki work and teachings is medication. In reality, he also used meditation on Gassho (hands kept in the posture of prayer) as a way to pass on the power to transmit Reiki to the learner of Reiki. Twenty years ago Osho Neo Reiki developed by Osho Neo included strong meditations for quicker healing.

Throughout Japan and other countries, a variety of Reiki Meditations types have made their way since Mikao Usui. The simplest and most effective RM consists of:

- Sit calmly in Sukh Asana with your eyes closed or straight on a chair, and hands placed on the chest front, in meditation 'Gassho' pose and feet sole linked together.

- By the simple intent connect to the Reiki or by drawing a distant symbol of healing.

the symbol of power is drawn in front with your hand, and three times say it. Visualize emitting white light from the eyes.

- Visualize and meditate on the icon in the 3rd eye chakra.

- Now cause the emblem to rise up over your crown as dazzling light. Your awareness is returned to the Chakra of the 3rd eye.

- Relax and unleash all your thoughts when finished. The healing energy makes you feel energized fully.

The Gassho meditation can be performed in this way for those who can't channel Reiki:

- Over the chest just Keep your hands in praying pose so that the exhaled air at the point can be heard where the tip of the mid finger reflecting the dimension of fire touch the linked hands together.

- Concentrate your mind now at that stage and seek to release scattered thoughts by continuously concentrating on the spot. Seek not to hunt away wandering feelings. Return the attention to the target by pushing one against the other two middle fingers.

For 20 mins a day practice RM or until there is a comfortable feeling. Meditation of Reiki deftly joins the common effects of healing of the techniques of simple meditation with Reiki and then works in several ways. RM twenty minutes a day, or as long as you feel at ease. Reiki Therapy skillfully blends with Reiki the normal calming benefits of basic mediation methods and functions in many respects than one.

Chapter 9: Reiki Aura Cleansing Secrets For Happiness In Life

You will share of your atmosphere with the dark clouds and refresh yourself with good energies of order to stay content in life. What exactly is an Aura, then?

Your Aura is a body of energy that encircles and permeates your physical body.

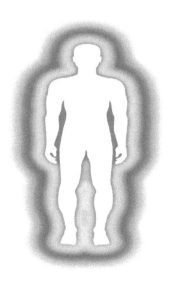

It's also where, in time and space, elusive stuff like feelings, perceptions and affection reside. As with your physical body, your Aura can be healthy or sick.

Bad energies will block your Aura and hamper your ability to act as a healthy person.

Cleaning your Aura helps you to:

- Think clearly
- Avoid or reverse chronic disability
- Open up to earthly love and to others throughout your life
- Undergo deep, restful sleep and reawake the body
- Give way to lost passions or ambitions
- Raise your spiritual link with the Divine and the Cosmos

Here are the ways of cleaning your Atmosphere and bringing joy into life:

9.1 Avoid People and Places with Bad Energy

Your Aura is not created entirely from your own material. Often, it consumes energy from the environment. All the individuals you associate with, and invest your time in locations. All of them have their own Auras which send out energy. You take the strength and you render it a part of your own Aura. It can cause negative energy blocks and chords in your own Aura and result in poor emotional, mental, physical, and spiritual health if you spend time around people or places that give off negative energy. On the other side, consider how you feel when you invest time with uplifting good energies surrounding men, or places. Your Aura is charged and you're feeling happy, healthy and in a high spirit.

9.2 Do a journaling exercise

On a sheet of paper you can make 2 columns. You should note down the individuals and locations on the left side that offer you the toughest feelings while you're with them, while on the right side you should note down the ones that offer you the strongest feelings. You'll notice very quickly that most of the bad items in your list have some things in common:

- People sometimes complain about others because don't have anything going on with their own life
- Most individuals are disorganized, frenzied or lose self-control.
- Their bodies experience detrimental energy signs such as alcohol, obesity or discomfort.

You may probably note certain trends in your list about the successful items:

- Inspired men, visit places and lead exciting lives.
- They radiate a sense of peace and transparency which makes you feel relaxed talking to them
- Throughout their life they tend to think deeply for you and other men.

If you've compiled your chart, now it's just a question of investing less time around the individuals and locations that make you feel sad and exhausted, and more time with those who make you feel satisfied and energized. If you schedule time to be in a positive environment on your calendar, it will help ensure that you are actually doing so. If it's not in your diary, so it's just sort of overlooked. Through completing this exercise you will begin to have more understanding regarding the life and PEACE OF MIND. But one more thing you have to do is stop negative energy building up in your Aura. You have to repair the energy coming from inside to yourself. Shift the Form of Conviction This is where it all starts. Your belief system is the source of your quality of life and health. Some explanations of beliefs include: "I am superior" or "I just have to take power. "On the seventh layer of your aura, your value structure resides and influences the well-being of all the layers below it. And if it's associated with the world reality, then it reflects positive health down into your aura layers and through your actual body. But if your belief system is flawed then disease spreads through your aura and leads to poor choices in life and physical illness.

7th Layer: Belief
Believes he must have control

6th Layer: Love
Loves having control

5th Layer: Will
Tries to have control

4th Layer: Desire
Desires to have control

3th Layer: Thought
Thinks he can have control,
or thinks he can't have control

2nd Layer: Emotion
Believes he must have control

1st Layer: Physical
Disease

So how do you align your system of beliefs to the universe?

You may begin by looking into your illness. You know that like suffering, sickness is the body's warning to avoid doing it.

What does the illness say to you, then? This is a really personal matter because everybody needs to understand for themselves or for their psychiatrist the nature of their disease.

If it's connected to being dependent on others, then you have to correct your system of beliefs. You will feel that the energy which radiates from within is pure and full of divine love.

Now, you have two things to ask yourself

1. What do you say by your disease or by undesirable condition?

2. How are you going to change your belief system?

Only consider carefully, since it depends on your life and health.

When you eliminate the hidden cause of toxic energies impacting your Auras, you will begin cleaning out the blockages that have formed up in it by performing the following.

9.3 Use Light Visualizations

The explanation why light visualizations are so good at clearing out the Aura is because they utilize Life Force Power to clear away toxic blockages. Visualization is an instrument that you can use to "move energy" every morning, before being overwhelmed by stuff like email and other tasks you need to do, you should perform the following light visualization.

1. Sit in a relaxed position, on the concrete, feet flat and arms in your lap.

2. Start breathing deeply for a few minutes, counting up to 5 at each breath and then starting again from 1. This will encourage you to relax and concentrate on your mind and body.

3. Seek visualizing white curing light that purifies the body and dissolves the toxic energies within you.

4. Then extend the light into your aura's first sheet, and let it sweep out all the blockages there. This move

will be replicated with all 7 layers of your aura, concentrating on any places you feel disconnected from.

5. You will then concentrate on the beautiful sense of being cleaned by the soothing sun for a few minutes.

That encompasses the practice of visualization. The next topic is how you use physical workouts to purify your Aura

9.4 Focus on your Physical Body

Our Auras are linked to our actual bodies, and one's wellbeing is related to another. An emphasis on actively removing your energy reserves is imperative for you. You may have a dark cloud of energies stuck in, for example, the Astral layer of your Aura (4th layer) because of an abusive relationship in your life with a certain entity. You can begin by folding your body backwards over a stool to free up the region where the cloud was trapped in your Aura. After a few minutes you'll notice the cloud rising in your palm from your right arm coming out of the smaller Chakra.

You'll think you've taken a weight off your shoulders ... because it literally was. This poor partnership can also build barriers that might disrupt your Earth link. You may retreat more and more into the spiritual realm to hide from your problems and this may even impede your goal fulfillment. You can take the person out of your life with this therapy and through their harmful effect on your Aura. Now it's time to return to earth. You will achieve so by using drills and gentle movements to strengthen the muscles. Within a matter of weeks, you'd see the blocks disappear. It's time to build a balanced flow of constructive energies into your body with the harmful energies eliminated from your Aura.

9.5 Repeat Reiki Treatment frequently

Here's another trick for purifying your Aura. You should use Reiki to unlock the Chakras and receive loads of good energies.

Your Chakras are the openings in your body that suck up the energy of life force and transmit it to your Aura and to the organs in your body.

Without a good flow of positive energy, creeping in on negative energy is simple.

About 20 minutes a day, you should perform Reiki exercises of your own, concentrating primarily of clearing up the Chakras, which feel clogged or unbalanced.

Some of the Chakras will usually start working after the first few sessions, although some of them can take a few weeks to completely open. As each must be restored, you can sense feelings that you have overlooked coming back to you. Your thinking is becoming sharper. You'll be a bit optimistic about living. Therefore you will create a deeper metaphysical bond with the cosmos. If you're Chakras drain energies efficiently into life power, your final move will be to go to a beautiful place of optimistic thoughts.

9.6 Reconnect with Nature

Human beings have lost their fundamental connection. We forget we're a member of nature. We waste our days looking at computer screens in workplaces, speeding along gravel roads in metal vehicles, and using robots to cook our meals. In a sense, these developments make our lives easier but we have overlooked that in order to be good human beings, we do need to remain true to nature. You could hear it. And if you don't (yet) have the gift of clairvoyance, you will experience the vivid good energy that comes from nature. It is so much life itself. Animals, trees, gravel, soil etc. Everyone gets their own Auras. By being close to nature you directly connect your Aura and absorb the positive life-giving energy that they send out into the world. Now that with Reiki you have already opened your Chakras, you can pull in loads of the strength.

Here are a few ways you can render nature a part of your everyday life:

- Building a landscape to meditate in
- Plant healthy, new crops
- Adorn your house with lots of plants
- Do yoga in woods or by pond

9.7 Some other techniques of Aura Cleansing with Reiki

Aura is the field of energy which surrounds any entity or individual. This energy field is formed by the body's power centers known as the chakras. When we send Reiki to oneself or someone, the energy field gets enhanced. Aura Cleansing is the way the toxic debris / energy is separated from one's aura.

Follow the procedure below:

1. Cover all the mirrors in the space where the aura cleaning should be done.

2. Sit on a chair / stool with the companion without adding any jewelry (except gold and silver)

3. Ask them to shut their doors, and to relax.

4. Put a bowl of water inside with salt from rock to the back. (Glass / plastic should be clear in bowl)

5. Gratitude disposition. Step up to your friend.

6. Draw the patterns on the chakra of their Head. Offer Reiki a while on the Crown Chakra. (Let us lead you through your intuition)

7. Shift your hands from shoulder to foot releasing aura ties to release the healing aura. (2 Updates)

8. Shift the hand at the aura stage from shoulder to legs concurrently chanting SHK. Visualize that you strip all the negativities off the atmosphere and brush it into the tank. Perform it 3 times.

9. Give the aura a loving touch, and seal the aura back. Both the words shout at the same moment.

10. Switch from the right hand to the partner's back and replicate measures 6-9 with the exception that cleaning takes place till the seat and not the foot.

11. From your right hand, move up center. Send Reiki to the Heart Chakra in a radius.

12. Project white light out of your hands. On your right hand 2 fingers draw 3 white light circles around the human. Looking into the partner's 3rd eye, display

all the patterns in the shading of the white light head to toe.

13. Sometimes send Reiki, throw the water into a basin, or flush it. Tell the person to come to reality, gradually.

Throughout the procedure you (even your clothes) shouldn't contact the customer at all point. Place a large mat below the chair or table to make it easy for the partner to walk around.

9.8 Additional Tips for Aura Cleansing

The "echo" is a rainbow-like electric force field that spreads throughout the human body and is adapted to our feelings, wellbeing and situations outside. This is a multicolored vision cover with several layers: the etheric body, the astral body, the emotional body, the deeper conceptual body, the metaphysical body and the casual body, each of which combined creates the illusion of a mixture of shades and light across the skin which becomes, ultimately, an expansion of the bodily self. Each of us has fields of energy that communicate with each other, which is why we often get those odd thoughts in the gut — such as thinking "I have a very poor feeling about it." It's our atmosphere that does the work. A multitude of individuals and circumstances will strip our auras from their potential: dysfunctional marriages, failed careers, family issues, and the twenty-first - century daily life encounters. We will get influenced by the world as well. Remember earlier in the year when you feel restless and uninspired? It'll definitely have been anything to do with Mars Retrograde and its impact on our energy balance. I had felt powerful, distracted and highly hormonal these past few days, and I knew it corresponded to the previous Super Moon, the night when the moon was near to Earth than it had been in over twenty years , culminating in a moon that was fourteen percent bigger and thirty percent stronger, the illusion of a stargazer. When you feel like your aura has drained out, is over-emotional, depressed, uninspired, pissed off at the sky, or just in a general rut, it might be time to start purifying your aura and restore it to its maximum, rainbow capacity. As such, a compilation of things you should use to help get the body, mind and spirit back to its core is as follows.

Walking in the rain

Forget where you need to go, what you need to achieve, and who you need to be, and just surrender yourself to cleanse of rainwater. It will enable nature to bathe your aura and neutralize any toxic, destructive energy that has messed with it. Visualize your worries and stresses away dripping from you like droplets of water, as you feel the rain on your skin. Yet remember: Don't move through a thunderstorm.

Cleanse your aura by smudging it with healing herbs

Smudging relates to the burning of herbs in traditionally shamanic rituals, where the smoldering plant emits a smoke that contains the plant's specific properties, enabling it to bathe and purify the atmosphere with its own communication. Getting more harmful feedback when we sense our aura strength is weaker, we will smudge our aura with the smoke from herbs with soothing powers, such as sage, juniper and lavender. Light your smudge stick and transfer the smoke over every aspect of your body, beginning with your feet going rising to your knees, chest, back, thighs, arms, and hands going eventually the heart, face and head. Notice the smoke spreading and flowing through the numerous areas of the body, helping the properties of the drug to cleanse the Higher Self and psychologically remove all tension from the force in the aura, as it does.

Take a cleansing bath

Cleaning baths are valuable tools to purify the atmosphere of all harmful energy, particularly baths with eucalyptus, sea salt and lavender to relax the body, mind and spirit. Soak for at least ten minutes and watch the water flow from the bathtub until finished, consciously visualizing all the aura-detrimental stuff that go down with the wash. If the auric signals are especially weak, a salt-water bath is suggested for better performance.

Visualize the auras of others

Take the time to envision other humans' auras, and even plants and animals. Mentally image auras originating from certain aspects of life to cultivate and enhance your own aura – visualize either a kaleidoscopic array of life-circling shades, or an extreme, pure white light. Note the colors that you use, and how they make you look.

Surround yourself with positive energies

It is necessary to be mindful of certain people / situations that sap our energy and reduce our capacity for aura. Therefore, restricting your access to the conditions that feed off your energy as frequently as possible is vital to your survival in order to maintain it safe and nourished. One must always note that, as coexisting beings, our auras touch, bind and engage with each other, indicating that we draw in the energies (both good and negative) of others. Hence, holding your aura near to you is necessary. To do so, just picture it circling you closely: lightweight and impenetrable. Your aura therefore intersects less with others which renders it less susceptible to outside powers.

Take a bath in sunlight

Spending too much time with nature in the sunlight is like honey to a flower, with the fragrance. It is understood that sunshine nurtures, stimulates and extends the atmosphere thereby nourishing the senses, helping you feel relaxed and even more positive and hopeful. Go to walk outside in the sunlight.

Strengthen your aura with a simple exercise

Find a peaceful place, and lie down quietly. Let your body and mind relax–let go of the stress and core of existence focus on yourself. Imagine your aura (its colorful rainbow and all of it) flipping right into the room corners, leaking out, lapping the walls. Then, gradually draw it back into yourself until it coils just centimeters from your surface and becomes impenetrable to outside influences. Repeat as much as it feels good. Use this again, but just let your aura move a small distance from the actual self (maybe a few metres) and draw it back towards yourself as before when you feel confident. Repeat this again as many times as you feel ought to. Ultimately, picture a rainbow of colors, your light lightweight, impenetrable, pulsating. At its most powerful this is your power. Practice to do so regularly. Perform this practice for at least one month and record shifts in your attitude, thoughts, feelings and daily encounters as a consequence of the strengthening senses of the aura.

Conclusion:

Over the past 15 to 20 years, there has been a considerable rise in curiosity in recovery, and this has been part of the explanation for the propagation of Reiki worldwide. Over the span of time, though, and particularly after the mid-1990s, the initial Reiki method in the West has adapted and expanded. As knowledge eventually came out of Japan in the late 1990s, both about Dr. Usui's true past and the healing system he began and about methods we did not recognize, this created considerable upheaval in several Reiki societies as it questioned their belief that "traditional Reiki" was what they were providing.

The condition is perhaps much more complicated today, since all the time, "new" Reiki healing systems are being created, often focused on the initial Usui Reiki, but adding new icons, distinct methods of tuning, and tons of new concepts. In addition to this, the arguments that one method is "better" than another and the other systems "just don't work" are counterclaimed, and it is very challenging to break through the dross and figure out what each system provides.

Since the term Reiki in Japanese can apply to any healing force, as I mentioned in an earlier chapter, most of these modern healing systems use the word to describe themselves and also, possibly, to benefit from the original Usui Reiki popularity, which is now well-known in almost all countries.

CPSIA information can be obtained
at www.ICGtesting.com
Printed in the USA
BVHW061003080221
599628BV00015B/1577